THE FICTION OF A THINKABLE WORLD

THE FICTION OF A THINKABLE WORLD

Body, Meaning, and the Culture of Capitalism

MICHAEL STEINBERG

MONTHLY REVIEW PRESS

New York

Library of Congress Cataloging-in-Publication Data

Steinberg, Michael, 1951-
   The fiction of a thinkable world : body, meaning, and the culture
   of capitalism / by Michael Steinberg.— 1st ed.
      p. cm.
   Includes bibliographical references and index.
   ISBN 1-58367-115-3 (pbk.) — ISBN 1-58367-116-1 (cloth)
1. Subjectivity—Social aspects. 2. Social sciences—Philosophy.
3. Subjectivity—Political aspects. 4. Political science—Philosophy.
I. Title.
   B841.6.S74 2005
   121'.4—dc22

                         2005000245

MONTHLY REVIEW PRESS
122 West 27th Street
New York, NY 10001
www.monthlyreview.org

10 9 8 7 6 5 4 3 2 1

Printed in Canada

CONTENTS

ACKNOWLEDGMENTS

I N FRENCH A MIDWIFE is a "wise woman"—*une sage-femme*. This book's long gestation and birth were assisted by three such wise women. It might never have been finished at all without the interest of my daughter, Sarah Falkner—a keen critic, advocate, and inspiration. To her I owe the idea of framing the argument as a series of essays. Even more important has been her powerfully articulate exploration of bodywork and the thought of the body. The most activist of our circle, the final section of this book is hers by right.

The middle section, in turn, is dedicated to Franlee Frank, bookseller and advisor. Her encouragement did, indeed, give me heart, and her knowledge of the publishing world has been as useful as her recommendations and criticism. And without my wife, Loret Gnivecki Steinberg, I would never have known enough to write even this much. She, too, has been a patient and perspicacious critic, at first through her blank (and totally justified) incomprehension of the earlier drafts, and later in her elaboration of many of these ideas in conversation and in her teaching and photography. So much of what is central to this book I learned through our relationship, and as a small token of my love I offer her the book's first section.

Other friends have been supportive in ways they may not have anticipated. A few words from Brian Schuth and Richard Kroll were quite enough to keep me going. So, too, was Frank Howard's delighted laughter on reading the first few chapters. And Justice Andrew Siracuse allowed me—his law clerk—an amazing amount of freedom and more time to read and write than I would likely have had in any university.

Andrew Nash at Monthly Review Press recognized what I was up to from an outline and a few sample chapters. He was more explicit about the scope of the project than I dared be, and thanks to the challenge in his response I knew much more clearly how the final section should run. Every conversation since has been a pleasure.

The first, deeply flawed draft of what eventually became this book was written many years ago, in London, Ontario. (How relieved I am now that it was never published!) For that valuable experience I owe thanks to Balasubramaniam (I hope I've remembered the spelling), Morley Gorsky, Kay Adair, and most especially Alice Anjo, who helped support a luxurious year of reading and writing.

Finally, I would like to pay homage to the shades of three people whose contribution, though clear enough to me, is indefinable in conventional terms: Donald Francis Tovey, Nikolai Medtner, and Simon Jeffes. To all I have mentioned and all whose names I have unforgivably omitted, my gratitude and thanks.

OVERTURE

T HIS IS A WORK OF SYNTHESIS, for which the time is
never ready. It contains generalizations which will need to be
nuanced, shaded, qualified, or—alas—rejected. It speaks
recklessly of the "West and the rest" and yields now and then to the
temptation of citing aspects of Chinese culture by way of contrast, thus
running the well-known risk of constituting China as a reified Other.

My plea in extenuation is that these sins were committed in pursuit of an idea. That idea, bluntly put, is that we think primarily with
our bodies. We are animals, though conscious ones, and at the level
of subpersonal neurological processes all of us—women, men, children, cats, dragonflies, starlings, woodchucks, and everything else
that responds to other things—participate in and are constituted by
our mutual interactions.

To live is to shape each other in this diverse, decentered but
common activity from which we cannot separate ourselves any
more than we can remove ourselves from our nerves, muscles,
bones, and internal organs. Conscious thought is only one part of
this activity. It emerges within the context of subpersonal cognition.
Instead of interpreting the "raw data" of a world outside of our
thought, it draws from and depends on the subpersonal, which provides it all it can ever know.

Human subjectivity, in the sense of agency, is a social, common, decentered, and transpersonal subject—an "intersubjective subject." In contrast, the subject of conscious experience is an individual and apparently isolated subject. The confusion of these two is a commonplace in the modern Western world, but it is a deeply and dangerously misleading error. It leads to the specious isolation of the individual and to the alienated reappearance of the thought of the body as the omniscient and demanding social world.

This rendition of experience as a dichotomy of individual and social grounds the institutions of liberal capitalism, which are justified by the fiction that each voter and each purchaser or laborer makes free choices from positions outside of a social process. Inner life and social structure thus reflect each other today with a precision and a completeness never seen before. The liberal capitalist order does not need the support of principles of religion or divine authority, or even of a higher rational necessity; overt ideology is subsumed into the form of experience itself.

For this reason, no critique that starts from the separation of the thinking subject can move away from the world that it hopes to criticize. In our transformed world all definitions or dreams of human happiness, no matter how radical or transgressive, carry with them the fatal divide between subject and object and between individual and other. Attacks that begin there can only interpret the existing world in different ways; they can never suggest how to change it.

The production of this specific form of experience is the overarching function of all institutions and social practices under capitalism. It can only be understood as something global and totalizing and can only be critiqued in the same way.

A work that tries to do this might pose an entire world against the one in which we now live. But such a monster could hardly avoid implying that it alone enshrined a theory that was immune to the problems found in all others. Any critique of a totalizing system of experience had better be an autocritique as well; so rather than a large, pretentious, and covertly inconsistent treatise I have chosen to suggest a comprehensive critique through the echoes, congruencies, conflicts, and resonances among the following essays.

For that reason, among others, this book attempts to construct a perspective point from which the world of our creation can be seen in a different light. It is the essence of a perspective point, though, that it is invisible to the person occupying it. It cannot be located or described. An author can do little more than point to one through the implications of certain arguments and insights, leaving it to the reader to take up the journey. Thus, as in Elgar's *Enigma* variations, "through and over the whole set another and larger theme 'goes' but is not played;" and that theme is the real subject of the work.

One justification for the multidisciplinary approach I have adopted is that it suggests several different paths towards that indescribable viewpoint. None of them refers directly to the others. The order in which the essays are presented is a deliberate one, though, and the implicit argument is best made out if they are read as arranged. The first group sets out some theoretical support for the centrality of bodily cognition, joining research in neuroscience and cognition with elements of the phenomenological tradition in philosophy. The next three chapters address aspects of the distinctive attitude toward conscious activity that has developed through western history, and the final group attempts to bring these themes together and show the progressive impoverishment of both inner life and social creativity that results from the separation of the thinking subject within liberal capitalism.

I refer along the way to biologists like Humberto Maturana, Francisco Varela, Richard Lewontin and Susan Oyama; philosophers Edmund Husserl, Ludwig Wittgenstein, and Susan Hurley; to historians such as Jean-Pierre Vernant, Peter Brown, and Caroline Walker Bynum; the sinologist François Jullien and the unclassifiable writer, filmmaker, and provocateur Guy Debord. If this book is not an exercise in eclecticism, it is because all these writers address aspects of its guiding ideas—but only aspects.

It is interdisciplinary for the same reason. The specialization of our university departments was not consciously designed to obscure the totalizing nature of the liberal capitalist world, but too slavish an obedience to disciplinary definitions would make it impossible to see the forest for the trees. So I have used notes only to identify quotations, written with as little jargon as I could manage, and tried to explain concepts so no glossary will be needed. I am forced to admit that the result is the kind of book only an amateur scholar would produce. My only real defense is that nobody else could do it.

THEME

God creates the animals; man creates himself.

—GEORG CHRISTOPH LICHTENBERG

Living systems are units of interactions; they exist in an ambiance. From a purely biological point of view they cannot be understood independently of that part of the ambiance with which they interact: the niche; nor can the niche be defined independently of the living system that specifies it.

—HUMBERTO MATURANA, "Biology of Cognition," p. 9

. . . in whatever way we may be conscious of the world as universal horizon, as coherent universe of existing objects, we, each, "I-the-man" and all of us together, belong to the world as living with one another in the world; and the world is our world, valid for our consciousness as existing precisely through this "living together."

—EDMUND HUSSERL, *The Crisis of European Sciences and Transcendental Philosophy*, p. 108

It is above all necessary to avoid once more establishing "society" as an abstraction over against the individual. The individual *is the social being*. His vital expression—even when it does not appear in the direct form of a *communal* expression, conceived in association with other men—is therefore an expression and confirmation of *social life*. Man's individual and species-life are not two *distinct things*, however much—and this is necessarily so—the mode of existence of individual life is a more *particular* or more *general* mode of the species-life, or species-life a more *particular* or more *general* individual life.

—KARL MARX, *Economic and Philosophical Manuscripts of 1844*

If change is to be understood at all it is necessary to abandon the view that objects are rigidly opposed to each other. It is necessary to elevate their interrelatedness and the interaction between these "relations" and the "objects" to the same plane of reality. The greater the distance from pure immediacy the larger the net encompassing the "relations," and the more complete the integration of the "objects" within the system of relations the sooner change will cease to be impenetrable and catastrophic, the sooner it will become comprehensible.

But this will only be true if the road beyond immediacy leads in the direction of greater concreteness. . .

—GEORG LUKÁCS, *History and Class Consciousness*

Don't look for anything behind the phenomena; they themselves are the theory.

—GOETHE

Therefore then, Subhuti, the Bodhisattva, the great being, should produce an unsupported thought, i.e., a thought that is nowhere supported, a thought unsupported by sights, sounds, smells, tastes, touchables, or mind-objects.

—*Diamond Sutra, 10c*

Philosophy is at once the power of alienated thought and the thought of alienated power, and as such it has never been able to emancipate itself from theology. The spectacle is the material reconstruction of the religious illusion. Not that its techniques have dispelled the religious mists in which human beings once located their own powers, the very powers that had been wrenched from them—but those cloud-enshrouded entities have now been brought down to earth. It is thus the most earthbound aspects of life that have become the most impenetrable and rarefied. The absolute denial of life, in the form of a fallacious paradise, is no longer projected onto the heavens, but finds its place instead within material life itself. The spectacle is hence a technological version of the exiling of human powers in a "world beyond" —and the perfection of separation *within* human beings.

—GUY DEBORD, *The Society of the Spectacle*, ¶ 20

Theories

1. WHAT IS THE HUMAN SUBJECT?

A HUMAN LIFE IN THE MODERN AGE appears to us as an immense accumulation of thoughts and actions. We are obviously bodies; but if we ask about the person who acts and makes a difference in the world—an agent, we might say— it seems that whatever we think about and see, hear, smell, taste, and touch during the course of a life is *our* experience, and a lifetime of thoughts, actions, emotions, and decisions, added up or summarized, is in some sense what we amount to as individuals. And this appears to be what we need to look at if we want to understand human experience and human activity.

In a commonsensical way this is the same conclusion arrived at by Descartes after long and terrifying doubt: that we know ourselves to be thinking beings:

> [W]hat is a thing which thinks? It is a thing that doubts, understands, [conceives], affirms, denies, wills, refuses; which also imagines and feels.[1]

But alas for Descartes, and for us also, this simple definition conceals many ambiguities.

What, after all, is "thinking"? It hardly seems to be as cut off from the rest of life as Descartes made it sound. Of course we doubt, understand, conceive, affirm, deny, will (in the sense of desire), refuse, imagine, and perceive—but we don't doubt in a vacuum or refuse when there's nothing to accept or reject. In a philosophical term given its current sense by Edmund Husserl, these are intentional states. Thinking is thinking-about.

Like Descartes, though, we usually see intentional states as relations between two different parts of the world. On the one hand there is thinking, which we do inside our heads. On the other is the stuff we think about, which is out there in the world. But this becomes a source of confusion very quickly. For example, a large chunk of our selves ends up "outside" instead of inside; witness Freud's conclusion that "in psychoanalysis there is no choice for us but to assert that mental processes are themselves unconscious, and to liken the perception of them by means of consciousness to the perception of the external world by means of the sense-organs."[2]

If we assume that the human subject is a part of our mental life that does conscious thinking, where does that leave the rest of us? It seems parsimonious to throw away our feelings as if they were less important than other mental events. And that is not the only problem that crops up when we identify ourselves with the subject of introspection. If we can be aware of our thinking processes themselves, it seems to follow that this thinking-about-thinking-about-stuff is somehow a higher or more central activity than just plain thinking. But if it is, what part of us is thinking *about that*?

There are some useful distinctions to be drawn along these lines, but this infinite regression suggests that separating thought and its object might be a mistake. If it is, though, the mistake is a common one, especially in the Western tradition. Freud's investigative consciousness resembles both the Cartesian thinking being and the image of the soul as charioteer in the *Phaedrus*, one of Plato's most enduring contributions to Western thought. The self or mind these claim to discern is an isolated intelligence lying not only within the body but within the thinking process itself.

Throughout the history of Western thought there has been a kind of historical retreat of the self into the recesses of the mind. Plato's psychology was a more private affair than the open thought-world of Homer, where the gods could grab your hair and fill you with courage or fear. Christianity laid greater stress on inner experience than the religions of pagan Rome, and Protestantism was more inward than most Catholicism of the time. In the past century this process has only accelerated, and the objectification of our own selves is such a commonplace that one finds books with titles like *The Mind: A User's Manual*. (Who, one wonders, is using what here?)

Perhaps we would do better with a different approach. Instead of joining another search deep into the self, let us look at where thinking comes from and what it concerns. This is something certain neurologists and cognitive scientists have addressed with increasing sophistication in the past twenty years. Their theories vary, but all of them begin with the premise that experience is somatic. Whether it is the twitch of a limb or the pang of heartache or the scent of a loved one's hair or the sound of a dog barking or the contemplation of ourself or of eternal truth, the site of our experience—all of it—is the body. We don't know anything that isn't a perturbation in our nervous system.

We consider certain neurological states to be sense perceptions. Others we deal with as introspective data. But we know ourselves the same way as we know the rest of the world, and our sense perceptions are just as much "inner" events as our emotions and our theories. Indeed, we sometimes have trouble deciding which is which, as Chuang Tzu did after his dream of being a butterfly, because the neurological events themselves do not distinguish between perception of an experience in the world "outside" and internal events.

What is more, experience isn't a matter of "raw feels." Even the simplest visual response is far from being the linear transmission of an image on the retina to a specific site in the brain. Instead, it is a process that brings millions of neurons in different locations into coordination, invoking an incalculable number of inquiries and associations. Deaf people who have received the controversial cochlear implants experience noise, but to "hear" they need extensive training and practice. People blind from birth whose eyesight has been restored have to learn to distinguish depth, shading, the edges of objects, and other aspects of vision that seem self-evident to the sighted but which are the result of an intricate complex of neurological processes that develop in infancy, at least in part in response to visual stimuli. Perceptions and introspection depend on a constant process of unconscious cognition, what Edmund Husserl in his lectures of the 1920s called passive syntheses.

Husserl was preoccupied with human mental life, but similar "unconscious cognition" is not an activity limited to human beings. Jellyfish have nothing other than a primitive neural net, but they keep their orientation and float at a consistent depth. It would be foolish to claim that jellyfish know they're upright or could tell us how far they are from the ocean's surface, but their behavior stipulates a preferred orientation and a preferred environment, and if the environment changes the jellyfish acts in response exactly as if it chose to do so. Viewed from the outside it is impossible to see this as anything other than cognitive activity. In the formulation of the theoretical biologists Humberto Maturana and Francisco Varela, "all doing is knowing, and all knowing is doing."

We don't have much in common with jellyfish, but we, too, depend much of the time on the same kind of knowledge. The greatest shock delivered by contemporary neurobiology and cognitive science was the news that we aren't conscious of most of what we do, that we don't seem to need consciousness for most of our everyday life, and that much of the time our conscious mind, which we think of as the guiding force in our lives, is simply along for the ride.

For example, we begin to move our arm before we think we have decided to do so. This is a bizarre result, to be sure, but it suggests that the mental processes we observe in ourselves when deciding to raise an arm are delayed reflections of something else that doesn't need conscious thinking at all. As one writer has put it, consciousness is always a few milliseconds late.

All of us do many quite sophisticated, complicated things without consciousness—not just breathing, playing the piano, or touch typing, but activities that require awareness and responsiveness like driving a car. Indeed, sometimes the most highly responsive states are those in which consciousness plays an insignificant role. A frequent memory of people involved in a disaster, often those whose acts are later seen as heroic, is that they were acting "on autopilot." They do what is necessary without making any conscious decisions, acting effortlessly and gracefully, their awareness content just to look on. (The theistically inclined will say that "something higher was working through me.") It's paradoxically easiest to achieve such a state of "optimal experience," in Mihayi Csikszentmihalyi's phrase, in the most life-threatening situations, where there is no time to ponder the next act; and this is perhaps one of the things that draw people to extreme sports, rescue parties, religious fasting, and warfare.

We can act without consciousness and even learn without it. Brain injuries that result in the loss of the ability to form new memories leave people frozen in time—the central character in the film *Memento* is an example. Patients have to be reintroduced to the doctor at every session. Yet even such severe injuries do not always keep these people from acquiring new skills. Some have been trained to do office tasks well enough to hold a job simply by being guided through the tasks over and over. At some point they learn the procedures, but they continue to deny any memory of the training sessions and any awareness of having learned anything new. They have added to their repertory of cognitive activities without "remembering" a thing.

These examples of unconscious knowledge and learning, which could easily be multiplied, suggest that the "folk psychology" that dominates popular ideas about thinking and even most cognitive science is a complete mystification of the way we live and think. In this model knowledge is seen as something stored up in a black box inside the brain. Our senses take in the world around us and send data to our blackbox-brain, where we choose a response. In more scientific-sounding jargon, this model assumes that there is a specialized region of the brain containing rules of interpretation, connected to nerves bringing it news from the outside and others, which carry marching orders to our arms and legs.

There is no evidence that this picture is accurate. Instead, both action and perception use a common network of nerves and brain centers. From the body's point of view seeing and doing are so closely linked that they are effectively the same thing, and to talk about them we are stuck with clumsy terms like action/perception complexes. Rather than being stored in some memory/decision module, knowledge exists in the state of those complexes.

We can easily see that the way we act depends on the way we perceive, but it turns out to be just as true that the way we see the world depends on how we act in it. In *Consciousness in Action* philosopher Susan Hurley explores this interdependence, contrasting it to the input/output model, and concludes:

> Perceptual distinctions and invariants and basic intentional distinctions and invariants emerge together from the complex dynamic system and constrain each other. To describe such a system as perceiving is to describe it as functioning to represent; to describe it as acting is to describe it as functioning to control. But *these are different ways of describing the same system.* And such a system's functions of representation and control do not in general map tidily onto a distinction between input and output. 3

Though this subpersonal knowledge does not exist in language or conscious image, it is accessible to us in a number of ways. The most common is the generalized awareness of our bodily condition that we call emotion. The association between these two is so intimate that William James argued that somatic states were identical with emotional ones; we do not run from a bear, heart pounding and breathless, because we are afraid; it is the urge to run, the pounding heart, and the gasping for breath that constitute the emotion of fear. (The contemporary neurologist Antonio Damasio holds a very similar view.)

James's position, while appealing, leaves no room for the complex interplay between conscious thinking and subpersonal thought. In particular, it makes it difficult to see how emotions can be *about* very much, or how the memory of a lover fills us with warmth or the fear of sudden death strikes us cold. But trying to keep the body out of thought is a more foolish mistake. Conscious reflection, thinking in words, doesn't get us as far as we usually think it should.

I want to know if I should leave my job and look for a new one. So I draw up lists of pros and cons: a promotion is unlikely until my supervisor retires, and she's only two years older than I am, but there is not as much demand in my field as there once was and I may have to relocate if I want to find a job at all; my wife will miss the next step in her pension accrual if she doesn't stay a few more years where she is, but she finds her job boring and might welcome an excuse for a change. I can write and speak millions of words on the subject, but it remains a very tough call.

And then, one day, the solution seems clear. As Laurie Anderson says, "Sometimes the answers just come in the mail." You know the answer because it has a kind of emotional luminosity. It just feels right. But who then is the sender? We say that we have a "gut feeling," and the metaphor points to an important point: we make the decision with our bodies, the seat of our emotional life. We do not decide with our (metaphorical) heads. Instead, we transcribe the message immanent in our flesh. Otherwise we can't make decisions at all.

Reasoning something out is, at best, an attempt to explain one's solution to one's self or to test it. It can't be confused with the process that it's testing or justifying. This is an experience familiar to artists, creative scientists, and everyone else who wrestles with genuinely complex questions, and it suggests that looking at life in a coldly rational manner is a kind of idiocy. In real life instead of *Star Trek* Mr. Spock would have been washed out of Starfleet Academy in his first week of classes. We are not thinking beings at all but bodies that think, and without the body thinking wanders into irrelevance.

Bodily knowledge is sometimes dismissed as "instinct." In one currently fashionable theory, instincts are thought to be self-contained genetic programs inherited from our evolutionary past that are present at birth and spring into action when triggered by environmental stimuli. But although there are predispositions "wired" into our nerves from the beginning—newborn babies avoid heights and are constantly sucking, for instance—biologists like Susan Oyama and Richard Lewontin have shown how misleading it is to identify any important part of our knowledge and conduct with the execution of a genetic program. Genes do not have any meaning apart from a particular life in a particular environment, and when these are altered the same gene's expression may change completely. Evolution is a continuous process whereby population and environment vary together. What is more, it did not end some time in the past, leaving the individual with a brain ready to cope with the contemporary environment. Instead, we can understand what animals do—including animals like ourselves—only as a continuing transformative interaction with each other and the world. Learning is not incidental to this process and does not facilitate it from the outside; it is this process.

Unlike the internal hydraulic drives of the Freudian model, the life of the body is part of an intricate weave of relations in which all things ceaselessly change each other. Its transformative interactions make no distinction between inner and outer or human and animal. There is no boundary within which we can point to a "me" apart from anything else. It is only when we isolate those parts of the process which we experience as conscious discourse, that we look to ourselves like separate beings.

The temptation to do this is so strong that we must remind ourselves constantly that discourse is not a discrete operation that reflects on bodily cognition from within. Conscious thought is wholly interwoven with the subpersonal. It necessarily appears to us as the interpretation of bodily states, but that is only because we cannot see the *unconscious* interpretive activity out of which it arises and into which it subsides. It is different from the rest of our cognitive activity only in its conscious presence, and though we can reflect upon our conscious thinking and reflect upon the reflective process itself, we should not take this to define any special status for consciousness with respect to subpersonal thought. Although it is almost impossible to avoid terms that suggest otherwise, it should be remembered throughout that the thoughts of which we are aware are merely partial and sometimes even random aspects of a larger complex of processes.

The intimate play of our interactions with all other beings brings personality "out in the open, where it belongs," to quote Hurley once more. Since our reflection is only an aspect of the life of the body, itself open to all things, there is no essence "inside" us where we can locate the self. Nor do we need to assume one to account for human individuality. Personality arises spontaneously, in the way our bodies speak their genetic and personal histories in the present. Those histories are nothing other than the acts of those before us and around us. The way in which we manifest them in our actions becomes part of the future we share with everyone else.

The world looks different for each of us, because we start from different points, have different experiences, and have different bodies that respond in various ways to similar events, but it is a *single* world. All of us are co-participants in the process that brings it forth and renews it.

Neither individual nor social worlds can be extracted from that process. It is thus dangerously misleading to speak of the social as a pre-existing transpersonal structure or *Weltanschauung* into which we are all socialized. Just as "nature" is experience after we remove whatever we have decided is specifically human, talk of a social world is just shorthand for human activity that isn't assigned to the essential self. But there is no essential self; the human subject is not an isolated percipient. Each of us is instead a unique node in a network of interactions, and there is nothing other than that network. You cannot cut off a fragment and say, this is mine; nor can you leave the rest and say that it is not.

What, then, of agency? Has it vanished inside a universal determinism? Not at all, because the process cannot be separated from its participants. It is not directed, because there is no point outside the system from which directions could come. But it is not static, either, because it is continually being reinvented by the actions of all who are alive. Agency is our fundamental activity, as we assimilate present to past and by every action make and remake the world together; only agency is something done in partnership with all sentient beings. Every decision is a kind of consensus.

This isn't the kind of agency we've come to expect, the lonely-at-the-top pondering of What Is To Be Done that goes on in the inner recesses of the soul. But it accords much more with the way our bodies work, and it opens the doors of our imagined isolation and shows us that we live in a world that is profoundly our own.

This is hardly the way our lives seem to us today. The Western tradition has placed all its bets on the separation of the thinking subject, and its stress on individual responsibility and the internal consistency of a self-generated personality shape not only the philosophies and psychological theories of the mainstream but most attempts to pose alternatives. Some of the most influential "critical thought" of the modern era does little more than follow this logic until the endlessly regressing self disappears into the vanishing point. This process begins most often with the identification of thought and language. What assumptions are concealed within that identification may be shown by tracing the paths from structuralism to post-structuralism.

Structuralists like Claude Lévi-Strauss and Roland Barthes began with the linguistic model proposed at the beginning of the twentieth century by Ferdinand Saussure. For Saussure the object of study was not the individual utterance or *parole* but the all-encompassing system of the language itself—*langue*. (The structure has to be all-encompassing because meaning is a function of differences within the system.) Structuralists admit that *langue* only exists as it is manifested in *parole*, and the two are said (by Barthes, among others) to exist in a dialectical relationship, but the only conceivable object of study remains the structure of *langue* itself, which assumes a fixed character:

> It is the social part of language, the individual cannot by himself create or modify it; it is essentially a collective contract which one must accept in its entirety if one wishes to communicate. Moreover, this social product is autonomous, like a game with its own rules, for it can be handled only after a period of learning.4

There can hardly be a clearer example of the tie between the association of thought and language on the one hand and the separation of the thinking mind from social process on the other. Even more clear is the way these preconceptions imply the powerlessness of the individual, who faces a Hobson's choice: accept the social order or resign from human existence.

From such a starting point one can only produce a history without subjects. The autonomous movement of structure can be grasped diachronically or its functioning mapped out synchronically; in either case the presuppositions of the inquiry leave out human activity. The late Pierre Bourdieu, reacting against this dilemma, mounted a sustained critique of the structuralist problematic. He pointed out that the gift exchanges that were so important in Kabyle culture could not be understood as aspects of a synchronic social structure. They were, instead, activities in which human beings created meaning in the context of a "logic of practice." The value of the initial gift compared with the response, the timing and manner of its delivery, the status of the givers and recipients—all of these played important roles in defining the nature of the exchange. What is more, at each step of the interaction the relationships involved were open to change. Each gift was an opportunity to redefine crucial aspects of the way villagers thought about and treated each other.

One could say that for Bourdieu a proper analysis showed us a world in which *everyone* is a subject. Accounts which present human exchanges as homeostatic mechanisms or as instantiations of a static structure obscure the lived realities of exchange and the ways in which they acquire and retain their significance.

The structuralist paradigm, though, continues to influence a great deal of contemporary thought. Even most of its critics share its assumption that language and thought are identical and the related separation of thinking subject from social activity. (Bourdieu himself referred to individuals "socialized" into a "habitus.") For Jean-François Lyotard, who was largely responsible for the term "postmodernism," language continued to constitute thought. What he rejected was the "structure" in structuralism, the notion of an all-embracing system. For Lyotard there was no single language in any culture, or at least those cultures subject to "the postmodern condition." There were instead separate islands of discourse, cut off from each other and existing in conflict or mutual incomprehension. At times Lyotard adopted Wittgenstein's phrase "language games" to describe these islands. Elsewhere he described postmodernity as the world left by the collapse of the grand narratives that had once served to unify thought. All that are left now are fragmentary little narratives.

Even the local consistency granted by Lyotard to individual language games or little narratives was rejected by Jacques Derrida. But Derrida also identified conscious activity with language. He attacked the illusion of "presence" implicit in folk psychology and the Western philosophical tradition. Since language does not, in fact, link to the world, its reference to anything outside itself must be an illusion; and since the neat binary oppositions on which the structuralists rested meaningfulness are equally ambiguous or delusional, the system is incoherent within itself. Humans, as beings defined by thinking and speaking, are solipsists—isolated minds blabbering in shreds of borrowed, polluted language about a world they can never really know. In fairness to Derrida, his own practice seemed to point to the wordless and the subpersonal, and his deconstructions were largely a way of clearing a space for the ethical to reemerge, somewhat in the spirit of Wittgenstein. Most of his academic followers, though, miss this point. For them there is no Archimedean fulcrum from which we can move the world; indeed, there isn't even a handhold on the slick face of discourse to keep us from skittering along its surface.

If anything is said to lie outside conscious discourse in these theories, it is generally modeled on the Freudian drives. For Jacques Lacan, for example, the unconscious was structured like a language, but it still bore all the marks of the violently antisocial desire found in Alexandre Kojève's peculiar and highly influential reading of Hegel and emerged only in the sporadic ruptures of consciousness. Agency, if it existed at all, was disruptive, chaotic, and generally impotent, much as it was for Michel Foucault, while the machinery of discourse and public life ground on regardless. (The day I wrote this I picked up a book by a postmodernist scholar, reading in a blurb that it discussed "the natural body that is the place of cultural inscriptions." This is common language in the field. I could hardly have made the implications of postmodern discourse any more obvious; the thinking subject, once the hero of social process, has been recast as the prisoner of Kafka's "In the Penal Colony.")

Behind all these variants lies the work of Martin Heidegger, the great if sometimes unacknowledged influence on virtually all French philosophy since the Second World War. Few of those who fell under its spell have been able to escape from the path Heidegger traced as he sought, through a long life of redefinitions, to reveal where meaningfulness is disclosed to an individual subject.

In Heidegger's early masterpiece, *Being and Time*, authentic life arises only within the single "Dasein" (a term Thomas Sheehan felicitously translates as "openness"), a person who has been individualized out of the world of the masses by resolute being-towards-death. If we as finite, historical beings are delivered over to history, the hope of *Being and Time*—a passionate attempt at escaping the world of modernity, democracy, and the everyday—is that history itself would be delivered over to the resolute, for whom vision and fate coincide:

> Once you grasp it, the finitude of your existence snatches you
> out of the endless multiplicity of readily available possibili-
> ties—comfort, sloughing off, taking things lightly—and
> delivers you to the simplicity of your *fate*.5

Such hopes no doubt led to Heidegger's Nazism, but they were as
unsustainable theoretically as they were politically. The "later" Heidegger emphasized more and more the apparently anonymous and
unpredictable history of the availability of Being itself. Language is
the record and vehicle of this history, and often comes close to
appearing as its very subject. In any form, this vision cannot escape
the passivity Heidegger himself expressed in the title of his valedic-
tory interview with *Der Spiegel*: "Only a god can save us." We are no
longer able to grasp and control fate. We are mere pawns, waiting
patiently if without hope for illumination from above. As Derrida's
followers and Foucault discovered, the destination is the one Yeats
saw in "The Second Coming:"

> The best lack all conviction, while the worst
> Are full of passionate intensity.

Happily, there is something other than discourse. Language and
conscious thinking do not link up with an external world, but there
is no need for them to do this. Nor is language a comprehensive
system into which all experience is parceled. Instead, we can speak
with others because our language arises within the embodied web
of cognition in which we are all embraided. Our utterances and our
diary notations are integral parts of a public activity, and they are
just as understandable (and as authentic and true) as a gesture, a
grimace, or an embrace.

We are not thinking beings but co-creators of a common subject.
In each of us the shared activity of bodily cognition supports and
surrounds reflective activity, and through each of us that collective
subject is transformed in an endless tangle of feedback loops. We

address and shape it as we constantly struggle to comprehend our own lives. Nothing is given to us with an interpretation already assigned; we do not really *know* that we are impatient or anxious or on the verge of falling in love. These are conclusions, not facts. I am short of breath, my legs and arms twitch, my eyes wander, and from these I decide that I am bored and anxious, or perhaps that I am lovesick, or maybe that I am just sick. I can always revise my conclusions and decide that I had been wrong when I thought so. Even if I stick to my original interpretation, though, the expectations arising from its associations shape the way I approach the future and in that way they become self-fulfilling prophecies. (Psychotherapy and much ritual turn this process to therapeutic ends.)

At least as important is the way our expectations affect others. Just as dogs are said to grow anxious and even dangerous in the presence of nervous humans, so the people we meet during the day respond to the subliminal cues that manifest our own interpretation of the situation. Their responses often appear to confirm the very expectations that called them forth to begin with, and in the case of someone with a tendency toward depression or violence this cycle of reinforcement can become a vicious circle.

But these circles can be beneficent, too. One of the best predictors for a long-term marriage is the ratio between pleasant and unpleasant interactions between spouses. If loving conversations outnumber acrimonious ones by a factor of four or five to one the chances are very good that the relationship will flourish. Surely what is involved here is the shaping of the physical sensations of proximity and conversation themselves—not some balance of rhetorical persuasion.

These eddies and currents move outward and inward at once. The wealth of human cultures all form and maintain themselves by similarly shaping and channeling expectations and experience. Styles of interaction and child rearing, economic relations, working conditions, household size, religious belief, attitudes toward sexuality and its expression, and much else are constituted this way. From the moment we leave the womb and are greeted by our elders we generate an understanding of how humans fit together and what is expected of us. The tenor of our physical interactions in childhood shapes the conscious and unconscious expectations and assumptions from which we elaborate our worlds. These, in turn, are part of the milieu in which our friends, lovers, and children make their way with us.

The picture of human nature we assemble varies in different cultures. A Plains Indian child, swaddled and placed outside the camp to learn from birth not to cry, likely experienced his or her body quite differently from the Nambikwara infants Lévi-Strauss knew in Brazil, who were constantly embraced and indulged. There can also be very different styles of interaction within any society divided by class or caste. One would not expect an upper-class boy in Edwardian England, virtually a stranger to his parents and to girls his age after a childhood of nannies and public schools, to have the same affective life as one from the working class.

The complexity of these interrelationships is apparent in any "social trait." Even an area as small and relatively homogenous as western Europe shows significant cultural variation. In Italy one speaks virtually nose to nose; in Scandinavia and Germany conversationalists keep a respectful distance. But it would be a mistake to think that Italians are socialized to repress their natural feelings of discomfort at close proximity, or that northerners repress a contrary longing for physical intimacy. We do not learn these things by discursively deriving rules of conduct that acquire affective color as they are internalized. The supposedly natural disposition, the cultural code, and the emotional colors of inner life all constitute each other, and all are perpetually in flux.

We recreate, reembody, and slowly transform the patterns of the life we are born into, and we also struggle to figure the transactions of our bodily life through discourse, internal monologue, and the discipline of artistic creation. Reflection, in a lover's embrace of the corporeal, forever seeks an adequate expression of processes that vary both of their own logic and in the act of interpretation, and

though these remain ungraspable they may, if we are lucky, return
the embrace in a widening spiral of inquiry and response.

The space between reflection and its bodily subject maintains the
possibility of social creativity and change, and the collapse of that
distance would imprison us in a sterile changelessness. It is the very
inadequacy of discourse that leaves the door open to its transformation. Yet throughout the history of the West we have identified ourselves more and more with a mythical isolated discursive mind. We
have refused to see the limits of the languages with which we claim
to map out the world, and we reject anything that carries the whiff of
the transformative currents of bodily life as a threat to the self we
have laboriously built and maintained. Why do we do this?

It is certainly telling that the retreat into the self is most marked
under capitalism, in which human beings exist economically as separate units that relate to each other as vendors and purchasers of
everything from toothpaste to labor to sex. The logic of possessive
economic theory and of liberal law and political theory, often founded on contractarian notions of liberty and obligation, yields the
phantasm of human isolation and self-determination that is today
all but universal. It is a world which, though constantly recreated by
all its inhabitants, "unfolds . . . as a pseudo-world apart, an object of
mere contemplation."[6] The experience of living as an isolated mind
is the phenomenal form of capitalism; and capitalism is all the more
powerful in that its ideology exists as a form of experience instead of
as a body of maxims and principles that can be refuted or ignored.

But this illusion is not simply imposed upon us. Our self-
identification with the isolated thinking subject draws strength from
our fear of the body and the transformations and dissolutions
through which it lives and to which it bears witness. We know that
we will die, and as we grow older we see how few of our accomplishments are built on anything more solid than sand. Through the constructed self, the specious verities of dogma and the solidity we pretend to achieve through discourse, we try to live in a world in which
suffering, aging, and death have no place. But these aspirations are

doomed, because change and death are written in and by the very bodies that we are.

The temptation to flee the realities of life is as inevitable as its promise is delusory. In ten thousand different ways we have sought a refuge in eternal truth, only to be expelled by yet another angel of mutability. It is better this way, because the paradise of thought is more like a prison:

> Beauty is momentary in the mind,
> The fitful tracing of a portal;
> But in the flesh it is immortal.
> (Wallace Stevens, "Peter Quince at the Clavier")

Really, not the mind or the soul but the flesh is perfect and divine. The body is never the same; it grows, flourishes, sickens and dies, precisely as it should and in tune with everything else; but the rebellious mind tries to stop it in its tracks or demands that it exhibit different sensations and different emotions. As corporeal beings we are bound up with the interchanges of all things. Only the mind, terrified of the death that our mutable flesh embraces, turns away from that commerce for the delusional pursuit of certainty or eternity. The structures it builds are doomed to collapse; yet we continue to build them, while all unnoticed we as actual physical people make and remake our lives in common self-constitution.

2. DO OUR PETS LOVE US?

for Loret

THE HUMANE SOCIETY in my home town sells bumper stickers that read, "Adopt a lifetime of love." When you live with "companion animals," as they're now called, it's easy to yield to this view of things. We are moved as well as charmed and delighted by a dog's tail-wagging dance of welcome and by the way a cat curls purring in the crook of an arm. Such interactions elicit our own love for our pets and suggest to us that in some way they reciprocate our feelings.

As soon as you set such things down in print, though, they look like the worst kind of anthropomorphizing sentimentality. The dog only appears to be happy to see us; her behavior in fact manifests relief from the boredom of being home alone and the anticipation of a walk. The cat is responding automatically to our warmth, executing a genetic program that evolved to draw kittens to the mother's teats for food and to other kittens to preserve body heat while sleeping. The preference pets have for our presence is nothing more than an association developed over time between the sight or smell of us and various pleasurable sensations. The most successful domesticated animals, in fact, are those whose own programming produces the behaviors we mistake for love. Stephen Budiansky, a writer for the *Atlantic Monthly*, puts the point succinctly:

> Just as we are genetically programmed to seek signs of love and loyalty, dogs are genetically programmed to exploit this foible of ours.

His article was titled, "Why Your Dog Pretends to Love You."

Of course, dogs are not so self-conscious as to feign affection; in his title Budiansky (or the headline writer) ascribes the same cognitive sophistication to dogs that the article denies them. Like all other animals except for some great apes (chimpanzees, orangutans, humans, bonobos), dogs fail the mirror test for self-awareness. They lack what is misleadingly called a theory of mind, which is the sense that others are beings like us with their own thoughts, beliefs, and emotions; and a theory of mind is necessary for empathy. How can you be said to love someone that you cannot even distinguish from yourself?

If our pets cannot recognize our separateness or have feelings specifically about us (or anything else), it might appear that their mental life is merely a bundle of instinctual mechanisms. These fallacious alternatives have framed the Western debate on animal minds for millennia. Cicero thought that animals had no feeling but pleasure, "and their every inclination is directed towards it."[1] This position was echoed centuries later by Kant, who argued that a hungry dog presented with food had no option but to eat. (An odd choice from which to generalize; clearly Kant never lived with a cat.) Plutarch, a lover of animals who may even have been a vegetarian, took the opposite view. He compiled anecdotes of animal intelligence, and wrote a charming dialogue in which one of Circe's pigs get the best of the wily Odysseus, arguing that animals observe the ethical precepts of natural law so punctiliously as to shame humans.

We are still apt to share the assumptions behind this disagreement, which are a group of apparently scientific metaphors sometimes referred to as the input/output model of mind. In this model thinking is something like a telephone switchboard. Perception is the transport of information from outside an organism into the interior space of its mental life. Memory is likened to a set of stored representations, which activate under appropriate stimuli to be compared with internal representations of the state of things outside. Once a close enough match is found a response program is initiated, and the perceived results of the action are then filed away in another pigeonhole.

This model has recently received a Darwinian refinement. Evolutionary pressures are said to endow each population with perceptual filters and a repertory of responses that have proven to work well in a particular environmental niche. We are thus born with the useful, time-tested programs that we execute throughout our life.

The theory of mind is considered to be one of these genetic programs, but it is not enough to account for self-consciousness and human agency. In traditional philosophical versions of this model the conscious mind is depicted as somehow standing outside the input/output process but capable of influencing it. Merely programmed responses are mechanical; it's theoretically possible to build an automaton that would reliably match perceptual inputs with appropriate responses, and those actions, while effective, would not be evidence of anyone "inside" that chooses a course of action. (A well-known argument along these lines is the "Chinese Room" hypothetical of John Searle.) The acts we call conscious or deliberate, in contrast, are acts of choice. We assume that we can somehow decide among alternatives presented during the perception–memory–action process. Without this power there would be neither genuine thought nor genuine love.

This is the underlying conceptual structure of Kantian ethics, for example, which places the will—that *ignis fatuus* of the West—in the role of the radically free actor/chooser. It sets the terms of the interminable squabbles over nature versus nurture and freedom versus determinism as well as the animal consciousness argument. (Dogmatic sociobiologists, for example, adhere to this paradigm and claim that other animals are automatons, and so are we.)

If it were possible to resolve these disputes by coming down on one side or another it ought to have happened by now. Happily, they fade once the traditional input/output picture of mind is abandoned, as it has been in the work of philosophers like Susan Hurley and Paul Griffiths, theorists of autopoietic systems like Humberto Maturana and the late Francisco Varela, and in the developmental systems biology associated with Susan Oyama, Richard Lewontin, and others.

Let us start instead with something that I hope is indisputable: Animals are sometimes unable to act. They look to us as if they were trying to arrive at a decision. I finish my morning dish of yogurt, fruit, and granola and set it beside the table, a ritual I have followed for more than a decade. Our three-month-old kitten jumps down to lick the bowl. One of our older cats watches, seemingly torn between pushing the kitten aside and waiting until she is finished. Sitting is pleasurable. Something about the white bowl on the floor signals food, but the kitten's posture, or perhaps the sound of another cat eating, suggests the possibility of conflict.

One does not have to posit any level of self-awareness to account for this indecision. My cat is not weighing different action–result paradigms stored in some interior mental space, trying to decide which course of action has a higher probability of maximizing his future happiness. There is no such "Cartesian theater," in Daniel Dennett's terms. Instead, he is caught up in at least three different perception/action loops, and for a moment none predominates.

We are stuck with terms like "perception/action" or "sensorimotor" because what we see depends on what we do, and vice versa. There is a demonstrable physiological foundation for this; neurons aren't grouped into different circuits for recognizing objects, for storing memories, and for response strategies. The same systems respond in both action and perception and in memory and performance. The neural complexes evoked were formed by similar events in the past. They encompass muscle memory and image memory and are suffused with affect—the physiological tone and associated muscular state that we read as emotion. It is quite likely, in fact, that these complexes grew historically around affective responses, which play a central role in individual survival. Significantly, these affective complexes appear to have had diverse evolutionary origins, which is one source for the complexity of our mental lives.

When such complexes conflict with each other action is impossible until one grows stronger and the others weaken, a process played out through attending to particular circumstances with more and more precision. One or another will prevail; unlike Buridan's ass, real animals do not expire through vacillation. For a short time, though, incompatible potential responses exist simultaneously, and my cat fairly vibrates with the tension. Then the nervous system's state collapses into one or the other, and he jumps for the bowl or turns to cleaning himself or watching the birds outside.

Instead of a progression from perception through decision to action, which moves from outside to inside and back out again, we find multiple dynamic feedback loops connecting motor/perceptual complexes with each other and the environment. Instead of an observer hiding inside the skin, looking out and calculating, we see in every biological community a pattern of mutual transformations in which any distinction between inner and outer worlds becomes impossible to maintain; nothing exists that does not participate in these changes. In Susan Hurley's words:

> The causal relations between nervous systems and environments are intricate and continuous. There is nothing specially oomphy about causal relations inside the skin, or inside the head, nothing specially capable of pushing or shoving. . . . [T]here is no magical causal boundary around persons. Viewed subpersonally, they are in principle transparent to causality.[2]

Moreover, these feedback networks unite organisms not only with their communities and their surroundings but with their histories as well. We animals do not compose ourselves. We make each other, but not just as we please; we do not do it under circumstances we choose but under those that we find, given and transmitted by our past and our surroundings. We are linked with our fellow creatures and with the environment which transforms with our acts. We are equally embedded in the past, as we express and alter our evolutionary and individual histories.

These processes effect the organism's self-constitution in complex, constantly varying intercourse with its milieu, rather than in a dialectic of self versus other or through the expression of a more or less fixed genetic inheritance. Organisms and environment are linked in a decentered, ongoing current of mutual transformation for which any kind of mechanistic metaphor is highly misleading.

Is that all that goes on? I suspect that this is all that is *necessary* to account for everything animals do—at least the ones who do not pass the self-awareness test. It is not even necessary for the responses to translate into experience, in the human sense; not all our affective responses reach consciousness, and it's quite possible that for many animals none do.

This is not to say that animals other than primates have no expectations or desires. They very clearly do. Our kitten, for example, expects a particular window with a good view of the birds outside to be open. If she finds it closed and sees me in the room she stares at me and meows. She also derives obvious pleasure from lying next to me on the bed, and at the same hour each night begins to follow me, sometimes hectoring me loudly until I shower and get under the covers.

These routines seem difficult to explain unless her mental universe includes time-spanning relations such as those among the window, windowsill, birdsong, and my opening the window. She presumably remembers times when my presence and her meow led to an open window, just as she appears to know that at a certain time I go upstairs to bed. But these memories are much more limited than ours. The kitten does not seek me out elsewhere in the house when she finds her favorite window closed, and even when nestled close to me on the comforter she can be elsewhere in an instant. The temporal range of her memory is short, and even reasonably complex connections are not invoked unless a number of similar elements are immediately present.

As Cicero suggested, "animals do not have emotions, though they do have similar behavior."[3] (Since for him emotions were factual judgments this statement is impossible to dispute in its proper context, and it is useful enough in our own.) The consistency with which animals seek out what appear to be pleasurable interactions or environments suggests that they possess a kind of generalized bodily awareness along with their fragmentary time-spanning memories. But there is no evidence for our kind of consciousness among non-primates. Thomas Nagel, in a well-known essay, asked what it would be like to be a bat; but this really begs the question. As others have responded, there may not be anything at all that constitutes the experience of being a bat, only a succession of states that the bat incarnates.

At the same time, this is not the reductionist (or, worse, "speciesist") position it might seem to be. In fact, it is not at all incompatible with sentimentality about lifetimes of love. To see why this is so we have to look at a few more implications of the developmental systems model sketched above.

We usually assume that all thinking is like reflection, something of which we have or could have conscious knowledge. As we have seen, though, this is too limited a definition. Like all other animals, we are thinking bodies. We incarnate knowledge of our environment as we bring forth and refine our responses to it. Our acts literally incorporate social, personal, and genetic history; all are present in the body that in hearing, seeing, and responding is continually transformed. These transformations and the knowledge they embody do not require any level of awareness. Reflection serves to turn some of the implicit comprehension of the flesh into explicit discourse, but the knowledge exists and is manifested in behavior whether it's explicit or purely embodied. Just because an organism cannot tell us what it knows doesn't mean that it knows nothing.

We are commonly insensitive to this embodied life, imagining ourselves to be minds that move the bodies they inhabit. It is rare for us to be taken aback by the recalcitrance and purposefulness of the body itself. But there is, happily, one great, familiar, and wonderfully illuminating exception to this rule—the exquisite disorder of falling in love.

Even for us Westerners, after all, love takes place in the heart rather than the head, that metaphorical heart which has reasons the head knows not. (How Pascal's saying could be translated into Chinese, where thinking is done by the heart, is a puzzle I leave to others.) This is one of those clichés that opens on the truth. Kierkegaard says somewhere that a lover who can give reasons for his passion does not love. His is a genuine insight, but he did not mean that love is either accidental or inexplicable. As anyone who has known romantic love can recall, the experience is deeply, extraordinarily purposeful. Lovers are drawn together with the force of gravity, a sensation attested to in the very phrase we use: we all but literally *fall* in love.

The luminous delight of mutual discovery is much more than some chemical haze thrown up by sexual attraction, though these are often mistaken for each other. The "honeymoon" of physical passion, facilitated by the hormone oxytocin, is both a goad and a reward for the abandonment of constraint that love engenders, and it surely helps strengthen those neural complexes that evoke a nimbus of pleasure in a transaction as simple as the touch of a loved one's hand. But sexual happiness in itself cannot account for the astonishing and unanticipated rightness of things—not just the lover's perfect gestures and answers and even scents but, miraculously, the fittingness of one's own previously clumsy and oafish maneuvers. Love gives us grace, and the steps we take toward each other are mutually choreographed with unerring precision.

We do not write the story of love; it writes us. This is part of its folklore. As I told a friend about the attraction I was beginning to feel for the woman who is now my wife, she smiled and advised me to "enjoy the process." The unconvinced will dismiss this as mere *folie à deux*, but the rest of us will look for an explanation.

Ethel Person, in her often eloquent *Dreams of Love and Fateful Encounters*, offers a modified Freudian interpretation of the transformative power of love: romantic passion returns us to the security of infancy—hence lovers' preference for baby talk—and allows us to renegotiate the key psychological crises of childhood and recompose the narratives of our lives. This would explain our tendency to seek others who resemble our parents, or who instead offer the chance to avoid all reminders of a hated and unforgotten childhood. (A psychologist friend once told me, with a sigh, "You either marry your mother or someone who isn't anything like your mother.")

Cuddling with a lover affords the delicious claustral intimacy of being a babe in arms, and in the deep confidence that one is loved some of the defensive stratagems of public life can be let go. Yet Person's analysis doesn't seem quite adequate. In particular, it fails to address convincingly how we find and fall in love with another. She ascribes to idealization, or, in an analogy she borrows from Stendhal, crystallization, like the salt crystals that beautify a twig thrown in a salt pond:

> For Stendhal, love is an act of the imagination. The fever of the imagination does for the loved one what the salt did for the bough; the loved one, like the bough, is transformed into an object of great beauty. "Crystallization" in love is that process by which the mind idealizes the beloved and discovers fresh perfections in her.[4]

The combination of idealization and the single-minded demand for reciprocation breaks through all defenses until both lovers open "to achieve real intimacy and mutuality."[5]

Idealization, though, does not account for the mysterious specificity of our desires. Before I met my future wife I had been drawn to a number of other photographers born in the late 1940s, women who seem now to have been intriguing mostly because they reminded me of someone I did not yet know. On "some enchanted evening" we catch a glimpse of a person whose physical bearing mysteriously communicates a deep and detailed harmony with our own being;

only later, astonished, do we discover how many childhood accidents, favorite books, most detested foods, tastes in landscape and personal quirks and choices we share. This, too, is folklore, at least as old as Aristophanes' famous tale in Plato's *Symposium* of the sundered half-beings seeking their other halves. The conviction that one's mate is preordained and possesses exactly the character that complements one's own is too common to pass without consideration.

Is this occult harmony merely an illusion, brought about by our own idealization of the beloved? The fact that many arranged marriages become love matches in the end might suggest so. But there is much more evidence against this deflationary theory. In spite of generations of old wives, it turns out *not* to be as easy to fall in love with a rich man as a poor one—quite aside from the oversupply of the latter. And the number of unhappy people who find someone to confirm their specific neuroses is large enough to be depressing, though as Tennyson said of the Carlyles, any other arrangement would result in four people being miserable instead of two.

Surely we do not choose our lovers at random, fastening on a few appealing characteristics found in an available mate and fantasizing the rest. Being loved in return is gratifying beyond words, but mutual idealization is a treacherous foundation for a genuine relationship. One runs the risk of breaking through the imagined perfections of the other and landing back on earth. Sex, role playing, and alcohol can be employed, but the sun rises sooner or later, you have to put everyday clothes back on eventually, and there's a limit to the amount of wine you can drink.

Instead, we fall in love through a mutual attentiveness so complete that it is also mutual vulnerability. We are animals capable of discourse, certainly the only ones so endowed; and most of our daily commerce is negotiated through language and representation. But the net of language is a coarse one. The particularity of each moment and each interaction is blurred as it is rendered into the narratives within which we make our home; people are just another nuisance, just another maiden aunt, just another buddy. But this obfuscation has its uses. With it we construct mental worlds that resist change, the inevitable decay and death that humans, also alone among animals, know to be the future. Longing for eternity—the dream of a world outside time—we build a self and an intellectual home as a refuge.

Most of the time we live within our own ideas of things, and it is rare for us to forego them and see, in Wallace Stevens's words in "The Snow Man," "Nothing that is not there and the nothing that is." Much of Buddhist meditation practice is devoted to the difficult task of letting one's thoughts pass away; how hard that turns out to be shows the depth of our attachment to the shelter of discourse. Creative work demands a similar discipline. As John Cage once told the painter Philip Guston,

> [w]hen you are working everybody is in your studio—your past, your friends, the art world and above all, your own ideas—all are there. But as you continue painting, they start leaving, one by one and you are left completely alone. Then, if you are lucky, you leave.

For most of us, though, the best chance to slough off our discursive and defensive constructions happens when we fall in love. The astonishing perceptiveness with which we find a mate is only possible because we look with truly opened eyes. Like Whitman's child who went forth every day and became whatever he saw, we put away our fear of change. Only then can we see and experience the currents of mutual transformation through which we live, responding with ever more complete perspicuity and spontaneity to the specific character of the moment.

Love more than any drug opens the doors of perception. The world seems lit with extraordinary clarity. It shows us others whose character and histories speak to our own; and it opens us up to the intricate profundities of a lifetime of growing together. The lover's vulnerability is as much cognitive as it is emotional—there is no useful distinction between these in any case—and through our openness to the presence of the beloved and our surrender to the embraidedness of this connection we become sensitive to the subtlest aspects of the other's being.

A splendid account of this process appeared once in Lynn Johnston's finely observed comic strip, "For Better or for Worse." High school friends Gordon and Tracey have no dates for the prom, so they go together. As they dance, Gordon suddenly notices Tracey's smile—funny, he reflects; he's never really seen the way she smiles before. At the same moment Tracey looks back, also with new eyes. They both think, in the same thought balloon, of course, "There's no way this feeling could be mutual;" but we know better. A few strips later Johnston shows Gordon back in class—floating just a few inches above the floor. Those lucky couples who find love in an arranged union must go through a similar discovery.

It is not that we idealize the beloved. It is just the opposite: we see him or her without any ideas getting in the way. We see them as god would, exactly as they are. This clear sight is itself part of the exhilaration of love, and it cannot be separated from love's transformative rapture, which is not intoxication with an idea of perfection but liberation from the judgments and expectations with which we maintain a fixed construction of the world and the self. There is even neurological evidence for this change.[6] In our trust of the beloved we no longer worry about what we will discover in ourselves or in our partner, and we consent with delight to the iridescent play of affect that alters at every touch and glance, timeless but never the same.

Love, as Wittgenstein said, is not a feeling but "something deeper, which merely manifests itself in the feeling,"[7] The effortlessness of lovers' commerce is not a specific affective response, nor is it maintained by a spiritual gift. It is the intimately responsive and perceptive cognition of the body, unimpeded by quotidian discursiveness, and because we gladly follow where the body leads we have the sense that love guides us rather than the opposite. Its luminous delight arises from our visceral recognition of the mutual self-constitution we share with all sentient beings. We are as graceful as cats, and as mindful and free from thought as they are.

None of us stays there long, of course, and thus the human experience of love is not so much a fixed emotion or state as it is a rhythmic ebb and flow. Other needs and desires, reflective knowledge and discourse all reassert themselves as we pass from timeless communion to the day's business and back again, from dark nights when one is better off alone to the longed-for renewal of delight, and from partings that are little deaths toward the specter of death itself. Human love, like beauty, is haunted by finitude and sorrow.

This experience is surely what Martin Buber invoked in *I and Thou*:

> The world which appears to you in this way is unreliable, for it appears always new to you, and you cannot take it by its word. It lacks density, for everything in it permeates everything else. It lacks duration, for it comes even when not called and vanishes even when you cling to it. It cannot be surveyed: if you try to make it surveyable, you lose it.[8]

Instead of a taste of the dialogue between humanity and a transcendent divinity, though, the experience points to the ecstatic interconnectedness of all things. When language fails it is not because it cannot grasp the spiritual, whatever that might be, but because there is no discourse adequate to the body.

If this most valuable of experiences is grounded in the bodily cognition we share with animals, what place is there for the rational structures thrown up in human discourse—aside from their undoubted instrumental value? In Chapter IV of *The Descent of Man* Darwin suggested that conscious reflection may have evolved to address an imbalance between the quiet and consistent desires of social life and more imperious drives like sex and hunger, an idea elaborated in Mary Midgley's *The Ethical Primate*. (It is important to add that this does not imply the superiority of one class of impulses over another.) Our decision-making would thus differ from a cat's primarily because we (and perhaps other apes) have developed additional feedback paths. These strengthen or weaken specific action/perception complexes through conscious recollection of prior experience and imaginative depiction of possible outcomes. The so-called theory of mind is one such complex. Through it our neighbors appear as beings like ourselves, not merely as purposeful but also as vulnerable. We are able to represent ourselves to ourselves, too, and maintaining images of who we are and how we would like to live builds up some of the most powerful of these specifically human (or primate) paths.

Rationality is one way of representing this additional system to ourselves. But it is not identical with it, and in fact recent neurological research confounds the common belief that rationality is our fundamental tool for decision-making. Antonio Damasio, in *Descartes' Error*, makes a convincing case that the final arbiter in any decision of importance remains an emotional one. Patients with prefrontal cortex damage, whose mental faculties are unimpaired except for a loss of affect, are afflicted with indecisiveness. In one case the patient

> had a normal ability to generate response options to social situations and to consider spontaneously the consequences of particular response options. He also had a capacity to conceptualize means to achieve social objectives, to predict the likely outcome of social situations, and to perform moral reasoning at an advanced developmental level.9

For all that, he was consistently unable to make up his mind, and the choices he did make in both his personal and professional lives were disastrous. Without the ability to "feel" which of several possible options was the right one, he was unable to use any of his considerable rational abilities. In other words, he could maintain the overt structures of conscious reflection, but the feedback loops into his affective action/perception complexes had failed, and even infinite reiterations could not lead one or another of these to prevail and issue in action. It seems that the Chinese have it right. It is indeed the heart where we do our thinking.

We do not think of ourselves as making all our decisions from the gut, as it were. In serious matters, especially, we fancy we are guided by reason, and unless we're hedonistic caricatures we will put aside what we see as our immediate desires and follow the course that we believe is proper or right. But how do we arrive at such decisions? If we are not coerced or fooled into acting, we may believe that the longer-term benefits of proper conduct will outweigh the immediate gratification we have foregone. Such prudentialist thinking plays a major role in conduct as different as dieting (a minute on the lips, a lifetime on the hips, as they say) and the more mechanical forms of religion. It is easy here to see the "reasonable" conduct as a kind of affective investment, putting off a small pleasure to secure greater happiness in the future. Reason is thus merely instrumental; we are still seeking a goal defined by its emotional appeal.

But even if we think we're doing the right thing "for its own sake" we are following a course defined by affect. We believe that everyone benefits from our acts and the example we set. Or we simply couldn't live with ourselves if we shirked our responsibilities. It is a matter of upholding an image of ourselves, an image of the way a human being should live. This is a practice far older than the emperor Marcus Aurelius, whose *Meditations* are the record of one man's aspiration to a particularly noble image:

> In the morning when you rise unwillingly, let this thought be present,—I am rising to do the work of a human being. Why then am I dissatisfied if I am going to do the things for which I exist and for which I was brought into the world? Or have I been made for this, to lie in the bed-clothes and keep myself warm? — But this is more pleasant.—Do you exist then to take your pleasure, and not at all for action or exertion? Do you not see the little plants, the little birds, the ants, the spiders, the bees working together to put in order their several parts of the universe? And are you unwilling to do the work of a human being, and do you not make haste to do that which is according to your nature?[10]

Our most common expression for this attitude is telling: If I didn't do the right thing, I couldn't look at myself in the mirror.

Yet our decision making, however dignified it may be by the way we picture it to ourselves, does not work differently from a cat's hesitation before a bowl of yogurt. Reason is fundamentally a way of experiencing a particular group of affective processes. A good critic but a poor master, it neither defines the ones it reflects nor embraces all such processes. Our rational and reflective abilities are hardly useless, but they serve best, perhaps, as a check on the decisions we do make, in the service of the affective image we maintain of what we hope to be. We can describe to ourselves what we are likely to avoid looking at, what past choices now seem to be opportunities for regret; we can discover a need to expand our felt environment through art, literature, music, and all the realms of the imagination. These and other practices can catch us short when we might be willing to substitute the partiality of a discursive formula—often in the service of a strong but transient impulse—for the open attentiveness and sensitivity of the body.

The philosopher and Chinese scholar A.C. Graham proposed something along these lines in his stimulating but little-known *Reason and Spontaneity: A New Solution to the Problem of Fact and Value*. The task of reason, as Graham saw it, was to ensure that we weren't ignoring experience and knowledge that bore on our spontaneous decision making. Its repeated command is simply to "be aware."

Self-awareness and the ability to interact with representations of ourselves and our world are central to human experience, and nobody is apt to doubt that because of this our experience is different from that of cats, dogs, and boll weevils. Our way of being in the world, though, is not so distinct. Self-consciousness is only a mode of experience and not a way of acting. As we can see from the decision-making process, which is not the exercise in rationality that it appears to be, what we think we are doing can be very different from what goes on in our nerves. We should not confuse experience with the processes that it reflects. (Hurley's insistence that most problems in the philosophy of mind arise from a confusion between content and the vehicles of content makes a very similar point.)

But if our actions are ultimately determined by affective processes, and we lack an isolated faculty capable of a reasoned choice among alternatives, aren't we merely complex machines, different from animals only in degree? Have we escaped from the alternatives criticized at the outset?

Those remain illusory. No living thing can be characterized as an automaton and none is an independent, radically free being. The decentered interactions of the biological world exhibit neither mechanical activity nor a multitude of independent minds, the false antinomies of the free will/determinism squabble.

The issues in that endless debate are genuine ones, but we most often look for the answers in the wrong places. We ask if our acts are self-generated or are determined from elsewhere. Because there is no "elsewhere" and no separable self, the question is meaningless.

But it *does* make sense to ask it about the entire network of networks of relations that is our world—the community through time and space of all of us, humans and nonhumans alike. And clearly there is nothing that shapes or guides that incomprehensibly complex affair. The life we are part of is unconstrained and radically free, and as we act on behalf of everyone, our actions partake of the free play of the whole.

This may neatly sidestep some of the more annoying issues from first-year philosophy class, but it seems to give us little help in answering the questions traditionally associated with ideas of freedom and constraint. If our actions are free only as part of a causal system in which we are totally enmeshed, on what basis can any of us be considered responsible for our actions? How do we ground ethical obligation?

We have lost very little, in fact; attempts to ground theories of ethics on reason have never proved to be as successful as advertised, and the character of our common experience itself provides a much more useful starting point. Our sense of responsibility does not derive from the resolution of technical questions of causation or the existence of a will, free or otherwise. It is another way we experience our embraidedness with others. It may well be stronger in us than in other animals because we are the only ones who spend our lives shrinking from that connection.

One manifestation of that embraidedness is our dependence on the happiness of those we care for. This is often castigated as an infantile regression or the remnant of a shame culture, to be out-grown and replaced by the inner-directed monitor of guilt. But it is a normal consequence of our understanding that others are woven together with ourselves—the theory of mind again, which is neither theoretical nor an exercise of imaginative identification but a direct affective reality, as neurologists are only now discovering. The physi-ological toll of living with another's disapproval is undeniable, and so is the euphoria of seeing ourselves in the eyes of a lover. This res-onance is strongest and most profound in the splendid amalgam of a loving relationship, but it is present in all relationships to some degree. As Mencius argued, to be human is—in part—to experience a spontaneous impulse of sympathy for a child in danger. We suffer and rejoice with others and they with us. It is an odd kind of ethics that ignores such things, and Western philosophy lost something when the Scottish school of moral sentiment fell into disrepute.

More than that, though: without responsibility our lives would be weightless. There is a decent evolutionary explanation for our need to feel connected with our acts. Like all other organisms, we strive to maintain our biological integrity. If conscious processes are involved in decision making at all—as opposed to being epiphenomenal, merely along for the ride—they must, for this reason, depict our acts as efficacious. We need to believe that what we do will make a differ-ence in what we perceive as the external world. If we don't own our actions we would have no reason to act; we would not think about the possibilities of action in any way that would contribute to our survival.

Any other conclusion would not only be dangerous; it would hard-ly fit with the importance that we give our own lives. Philosophical debates aside, our ownership of our acts and their foreseeable consequences are given rather than being conclusions. They are unavoidable aspects of being conscious—though nobody would genuinely want to avoid them—and because we are so deeply embraided with others we similarly cannot escape our responsibility for the way we act with them.

So it is necessary as well as appropriate that the emotional foundation of our decision-making processes turn us not toward egotism but toward the subpersonal processes that we share with all beings. These come most to awareness in our experience of love, which calls us to the fullest experience of our interconnections and to the basic character of our being; in the words of Humberto Maturana and Gerda Verden-Zoller, "Love is not a virtue, indeed love is nothing special, it is only the fundament of our human existence as the kind of primates that we are."[11]

In the West, especially, we have tried to fence in what is often seen as the disruptive and dangerous force of sexual passion by denigrating it as "animal." But the grounding for our emotional lives and of our ethical existence as mutually dependent mortal beings is no less animal and corporeal. Love turns us toward that grounding, and what happens to us in love is what happens with all other animals; it is only different in the context of our self-consciousness.

Afraid of change and of death, we are persistently drawn away from the ceaseless transformations of bodily life into the delusory shelter of discourse, so often justified by the supposed primacy of reason. Love turns us back again, toward attentiveness and openness. Our pets, though, do not need to be led back. They are always fully aware, always present, free from the overgeneralizing defensiveness of discourse. Do they love us? In the fully human sense, with the care and solicitude that come from being social animals and from knowing our solitude, our mutuality, and the hard fact that whatever delight we have together is fated to vanish, cats and dogs are completely incapable of love; our feelings are not theirs. But they are no strangers to the state of deep and attentive connection and offer no resistance to the endless changes of life. They are tied to us in the consistent embraidedness of our mutual lives, and just as we and our lovers grow together through a lifetime of attention and transformation so, too, do we and our animals. They are not such bad examples after all.

3. COGNITIVE SCIENTISTS
AND PHILOSOPHERS

MODELS HELP US MAKE SENSE OF THINGS, and those closest to hand are the models of our own creations. The body as a machine is a metaphor at least as old as the ancient Greeks, who saw Archimedean levers in the limbs and a radiator for overheated blood in the brain. It has never lost its vitality, though the specific machines we talk about change with time. In 1748 de La Mettrie, in his notorious *Man a Machine*, pictured humans (and other animals) as the spring-wound automatons that fascinated his age, though his images got confused as soon he tried to elaborate on them:

> The human body is a machine which winds its own springs.
> It is the living image of perpetual movement. Nourishment
> keeps up the movement which fever excites. Without food,
> the soul pines away, goes mad, and dies exhausted. The soul
> is a taper whose light flares up the moment before it goes
> out. But nourish the body, pour into its veins life-giving juices
> and strong liquors, and then the soul grows strong. . .

In our day, of course, the prevailing metaphor for human thought and action is the computer.

In fact, the progenitors of cognitive science, that group of contemporary disciplines devoted to the study of the mind, were computer scientists. Just how closely the two were connected at birth may be surprising. Both originated in secret military work on machine–user integration, as Paul Edwards noted in *The Closed World*. The cognitive science program was first outlined in *The Computer and the Brain*, published in 1956 by the mathematician and cyberneticist John von Neumann, and ever since the computer has been the master metaphor within the field. As Howard Gardner says, "it is possible to be a cognitive scientist without loving the computer; but in practice, skepticism about computers generally leads to skepticism about cognitive science."[1]

It should be no surprise, then, that the prevailing orthodoxy in cognitive science is the "computational" theory, which with a nod to Steven Pinker can be called the Standard Cognitive Science Model. (I shall refer to the various divisions inaccurately but conveniently as if they were a single discipline.) A current textbook—always a reliable source of conventional wisdom—explains that

> [t]he computer is a powerful metaphor for cognitive neuro-
> science. Both the brain and the computer are impressive pro-
> cessing machines, capable of representing and processing
> large amounts of information.[2]

But in what sense is the brain an "information processing machine"?

Such a metaphor constrains what we can say about mental activity in several ways. It leads us to pass over things like emotional states, movements, body sense, and pains and pleasures. These can be input to the "machine" only as subjects or objects of quasi-propositional statements, and are thus either ignored or assimilated to language-like activity. And thought itself is interpreted as an activity carried out on internalized symbols. In other words, the model of brains as processors of information brings with it the assumption that what brains work with are symbolic representations of other things—objects in the world, ideas, bodily states, and so on—that are transported to a language-like faculty from somewhere else.

The same textbook can therefore explain mental operations this way:

> A basic assumption of cognitive psychology is that tasks are composed of a set of mental operations. Mental operations involve taking a representation as an input, performing some sort of process on the input, and then producing a new representation, or output. Thus, mental operations are processes that generate, elaborate upon or manipulate mental representations.[3]

This is the Standard Cognitive Science Model in a nutshell. It would be easy to show similar definitions in the work of most mainstream cognitive scientists, and accounts in the popular press assume it as if it were both obvious and true.

It is certainly obvious. Representationalism seems to be a perfect description of how I think. I have ideas *of* things and ideas *about* things, and more often than not I associate an image, a word, or a sound with these ideas: a cat or a picture of a cat, let's say, or the Battle of Marengo or a phrase from a late Beethoven sonata. Even those who draw a distinction between thought and language will admit that they think most of the time in language, the symbolic medium par excellence, and many who do not think in words, like the autistic Temple Grandin, are apt to look for concrete visual images to guide and memorialize their thoughts. This seems like proof, if proof were needed, that our mental processes cry out for symbols: if we are unable to make use of one type of symbol we seize on another.

The appeal of the Standard Cognitive Science Model also borrows heavily from the reputation of the linguistics of Noam Chomsky, who is generally believed to have converted a minor and slightly disreputable branch of the humanities into a Real Science. Chomsky himself was closely associated, at the outset, with the cognitive psychology that emerged from World War Two–era machine-user studies. He began with the assumption that utterances are generated from thought by applying a small body of grammatical rules to a learned vocabulary. He went on to assert that the linguistic environment of children is too limited and defective to account for their reliable acquisition of these rules; grammar must therefore be innate. He concluded that humans have a built-in Language Acquisition Device in the brain, a specialized module that, as some have noted, is better termed a Grammar Acquisition Device. Chomsky suggested that if we could understand the structure of this device, we would know something of how the mind really works.

It is this part of Chomsky's program that has had the greatest impact on the goals of cognitive science. The language module has been joined in the cognitive science field by a proliferation of others, such as the Face Recognition Module and the Theory of Mind Module. Today's sophisticated version of the Standard Cognitive Science Model is that the brain consists of many of these semiautonomous parts. Some parts manage input through perceptual interpretation—like edge detection and figure/ground analysis—and may also generate output signals for motor activity. Others are devoted to higher-level symbolic processing. Most (though not all) of these theorists postulate a Central Processing Module, which coordinates the more specialized modules and sends output to the language module for inner and outer speech and to input/output systems for action.

The model for all these units is Chomsky's Language Acquisition Device. To give one example, the linguist Ray Jackendoff, in an account of his thought tailored for a wide audience, maintains that

> the characteristics of the human mind revealed by language apply to other aspects of the mind as well—. . . language is but one example of a broader human nature. . . [e.g.]
>
> 1. Our thoughts are built out of a finite set of unconscious patterns which give us the potential for thinking an infinite number of thoughts of indefinite complexity.

2. These patterns in turn are constructed from an innate Universal Grammar of concepts. . .

3. Our way of understanding the world—including our way of learning about the world—is a consequence of this unconscious organization. . .4

Jackendoff and philosopher Jerry Fodor assert that all cognition proceeds in an internal language they call "mentalese," which is translated into English, Tagalog, Farsi, or whatever for both inner and outer speech. This would presumably be the language of any Central Processing Module. (Perhaps, being innate and therefore universal, it was also the spoken language of humanity before the Tower of Babel.)

But is language such a fitting exemplar for the rest of the mind's work? There are reasons to doubt it. In the Standard Cognitive Science Model language is assimilated to grammar; vocabulary is clearly acquired from the environment and is thus not part of the language acquisition module. And grammar has some unusual aspects. It can be adequately modeled as a finite body of rules—though adequate modeling does not imply knowledge of causes—and it is therefore something in which we acquire a competence.

Our knowledge of grammar, in other words, eventually exists in a static, final state. Once we've learned to speak "correctly" we don't get more grammatical. This sets speech, when viewed as grammatical performance, apart from many other human activities. We certainly achieve a level of competence in muscular control and then, barring mishaps, maintain it for most of our lives; but those who pay close attention to their movements—athletes, dancers, musicians—are always refining and perfecting their powers, often sensing that though physical strength declines their knowledge of their bodies continues to grow. But this is as close as anything else gets to a parallel with grammar. Writers do not expand their grammatical powers as their command of the language increases. Nor can art, cooking, crime detection, lawyering, medicine, acting, horse-training, or love be learned as a circumscribed body of thought or practice.

Taking grammar as the model for mental life leads to several unforeseen consequences that reveal the hidden presuppositions of the Standard Cognitive Science Model. Whatever role the child's environment plays in the acquisition of grammar—the preferred interpretation is that at most it stimulates the inherent growth of innate rules—it is a temporary one. The social world is seen as something we grow out of, like training wheels on a bicycle. Once the grammatical faculty has matured the environment is strictly unnecessary; the learner leaves the social milieu like a child leaving home. This follows not from the innateness hypothesis but from grammar's being a competence.

If this is the way the rest of our minds work, we are separate, independent beings whose mental activities consist of analyzing, interpreting, comparing, choosing, and acting. We depend on others to teach (or evoke within us) those bodies of rules that allow us to carry out these activities efficiently. That is as far as our common life goes. Our mental tools having been honed, we employ them throughout adulthood as we look at the world "outside" and choose the actions we wish to pursue in it.

This is a classically Cartesian model: it implies both atomistic individualism and a simplistic epistemological realism. The world is accepted as given to us, with reasonable accuracy, through our senses. We are radically apart from that world and from each other. Our endowments are internal and fixed, like those of Leibniz's window-less monads. The only difference is that we attribute any preexisting harmony to natural selection instead of to Leibniz's god.

We are not compelled to this conclusion. A belief that language can be adequately understood as the manipulation of symbols according to a finite body of rules does not imply that all mental activity can be treated similarly. In spite of Chomsky's great rhetorical skills and love of debate, his theories have never won universal adherence among linguists, and the actual results of Chomskian linguistics have never quite lived up to its promise. Even if we accept the existence of a Language Acquisition Device, there is no reason to assume that our other mental operations are the manipulation of symbols just because certain higher-order conscious processes can be modeled that way.

Neurobiologist Gerald Edelman, long one of the main opponents of representational theories, recently summed up the case in a book cowritten with his colleague Giulio Tononi:

> [S]ignals from the world do not generally represent a coded input. Instead, they are potentially ambiguous, are context-dependent, and are not necessarily adorned by prior judgments of their significance. . . . Representation implies symbolic activity, an activity that is certainly at the center of our semantic and syntactical language skills. It is no wonder that . . . we are tempted to say that the brain represents. The flaws in yielding to this temptation, however, are obvious: There is no precoded message in the signal, no structures capable of the high-precision storage of a code, no judge in nature to provide decisions on alternative patterns, and no homunculus in the head to read a message.[5]

The symbolic operations of language are a misleading metaphor for the much more complex work of the "lower faculties." In the words of a deceptively obtuse-sounding comment of Wittgenstein's—a favorite passage of the French philosopher Jean-Luc Petit,

> No supposition seems to me more natural than that there is no process in the brain correlated with associating or with thinking; so that it would be impossible to read off thought-processes from brain-processes. I mean this: if I talk or write there is, I assume, a system of impulses going out from my brain and correlated with my spoken or written thoughts. But why should the system continue in the direction of the centre? . . .[6]

There is a different current in cognitive science that suggests, in fact, that the "higher faculties" are themselves misunderstood as symbol manipulation.

Even at a relatively high level of abstraction the representational interpretation of thought runs into problems, though this is too complex a subject for an essay of this size. The nonconscious activities of the mind present additional difficulties. Since they are not conscious, how can we observe them? We cannot see them directly, of course; but even without the latest form of brain imaging it is possible to deduce their existence and some of their functioning. This was, in effect, the project of the early twentieth-century philosopher Edmund Husserl, and for this reason his work has received increasing attention from neurologists and cognitive scientists. Its insights and its limitations are both illuminating.

Husserl remains something of an odd man out in the history of philosophy. In English-speaking countries, especially, he is often viewed as a figure of historical interest only, a precursor to Heidegger. This is both inaccurate and unfair; in many ways Husserl's work is more radical than his former assistant's. In fact, it was far more radical than Husserl himself originally thought, and over a long career he was constantly revising and developing his ideas. He would work on half a dozen projects at once, and progress in any one of them would lead him to rethink all the others. As a result, much of his most valuable work is buried in the forty-five thousand pages of notes, most of it in shorthand, that he left at his death.

These continuous transformations create problems for those who would interpret Husserl's thought. So, too, does his vocabulary. His announced aims and his language are very much of his period: "transcendental phenomenology" aims at providing an unshakable—"apodictic"— foundation for all knowledge, establishing philosophy as the "rigorous science" it is meant to be. It is easy to mistake him for the pose he assumes in his photographs, every inch the ornament of the Universities of Göttingen and Freiburg.

Behind the beard and the equally rebarbative style, though, was the soul of a visionary. Husserl was born in 1859, three years after Freud, and died in 1938, one year before Freud's death. He, too, was born Jewish, though unlike Freud, Husserl and his wife converted to

Protestantism. His first major work, the two-volume *Logical Investigations*, appeared in 1900, the same year that saw Freud's *Interpretation of Dreams*, and like Freud's masterwork it tries to show how much hidden work goes into the world of thought and behavior that we usually take for granted.

Husserl's method, though, was completely different. His starting point was not the diagnosis of nervous disorders but the age-old problem of knowledge: what can we know with certainty? He could see that previous attempts to answer this question, from Descartes through Kant, Hegel, and the neo-Kantians of the late nineteenth century, had all failed, and he concluded that their error lay in failing to ask how knowledge *itself* was possible. The "phenomenological turn" of Husserl's work involves a shift from the question, "*what* can we know?" to the question, "*how* do we know?"

Many of Husserl's contemporaries had claimed for philosophy the task of studying the procedures of the other disciplines. Husserl did not disagree, but he thought that this other question had to be answered first. He wanted to understand the process whereby the notion of reality itself became not only evident but unshakable:

> [O]ur interest [is] exclusively and constantly directed toward *how*, throughout the alteration of relative validities, subjective appearances, and opinions, the coherent, universal validity *world—the* world—comes into being for us; how, that is, there arises in us the constant consciousness of the universal existence, of the universal horizon, of real, actually existing objects. . .7

Until we have a clear understanding of the way in which we know things, it would be premature to decide for one view or another. Every theoretical question, then, is "bracketed." It was not Husserl's concern to decide even the most essential questions, such as the existence of a world apart from our thoughts or even the existence of a thinker behind them.

This suspension of belief, which Husserl called the phenomenological reduction or *epoché*, focuses attention instead on the way we perceive and experience the world. The objects of the world seem "given" to us; they stand out "in the natural attitude" as if they were unitary objects. Yet we never actually *see* objects. The phenomenological attention to *how* rather than *what* helps us notice that we see only parts of objects, one facet at a time, badly-lit one moment and drenched in sunshine the next. Somehow we bring all these adumbrations or aspects together, and each time we see one of these fragments it seems completely natural to claim that we've seen the thing itself. In Husserl's words, we have "consciousness not of a changing multiplicity but rather of one and the same object that is variously presented."[8]

Perception itself seems to bring all these different profiles into a unity. We don't reason this out, any more than we need to test the confidence we have that there exist solid objects in three-dimensional space. What is more, perception embodies the further confidence that these objects persist. Within each moment we have not just a perception of an object in the present, but a "protention" of the object into the future and a retention of it into the past. (These are immediate characteristics of perception, different from memory or imaginative expectation.) We make a world that only *seems* given to us, and of course "we" are similar accomplishments; as Husserl wrote, "consciousness itself is no less given to consciousness."[9]

Neurologists, who spend at least part of the time poking around real brains, have increasingly been drawn to phenomenological theories as alternatives to the Standard Cognitive Science Model. At a neurological level the Language Acquisition Module is as invisible as a word of mentalese. The staggering complexity of the brain, usually considered the most complex thing in the known universe, is not reduced by any compartmentalization into parts for language, for walking, for tasting and smelling, or for thinking about a vacation in Aruba. Even the simplest perceptual act triggers activity widely distributed around the brain.

What is more, it is clear now that the distinction drawn by most cognitive scientists between sensory and motor activities is a mistake. The brain areas involved in perception are so intimately connected with those for action that they are better understood as unitary sensorimotor systems organized around activity and affect. We create our concepts in action, not through observation and analysis. (This is a process one can see in children's play.) Things have meaning in the way we relate to them and use them. It is our ability to survive and flourish that makes us successful animals, and our knowledge is measured not by stored heuristics but by the detailed specificity with which we can act in different circumstances. Looking, thinking, and acting are different aspects of a single process. It is simple dogmatism to claim that they must be carried out through the manipulation of symbols.

These insights find numerous parallels in Husserl's thought. His phenomenology is often stereotyped as static and dominated by the sense of sight. In fact, his theories moved ever closer to a grasp of the active, temporal and social nature of thought. He had started with the insight that perception is a process that links consciousness with the object. The sense of objects is not merely that they are given; they are given *for me*, and their existence is also their meaningfulness. The identity of these two is the key to Husserl's insistence that perception is fundamentally intentional:

> [E]very conscious process is, in itself, consciousness *of* such and such, regardless of what the actuality status of this objective such-and-such may be . . . Each *cogito*, each conscious process, we may also say, "means" something or other and bears in itself, in the manner peculiar to the *meant*, its particular *cogitatum*. . . . Conscious processes are also called *intentional*; but then the word intentionality signifies nothing else than this universal fundamental property of consciousness: to be consciousness *of* something; as a *cogito*, to bear within itself its *cogitatum*.[10]

Husserl sometimes referred to his thought as a form of idealism, but it is not the kind of idealism that insists that only the mental world truly exists. For Husserl, subject and object were aspects of a single process. "[W]e do not experience the object and beside it the intentional experience directed upon it," he had written in the fifth of the *Logical Investigations*, "*only one thing is present, the intentional experience*, whose essential descriptive character is the intention in question."[11]

We and our world would not be here without us; there would be matter but no "world." But it is equally mistaken to think that these are things we create on our own. They are built in the constant flow of connections uniting us and our world, and we carry out these fundamental constitutive acts constantly and invisibly. This process is both corporeal and social.

As his thought developed Husserl stressed more and more that not passive contemplation but understanding and use are basic to thought. These processes are profoundly rooted in our bodies, rather than in the operations of an abstracted mind, and bodily activity is what constitutes both world and ego. In his late writing he stressed the centrality of movement to our sense of objects, an observation that fits well with the idea of unitary sensorimotor systems:

> All kinestheses, each being an "I move," "I do," [etc.] are bound together in a comprehensive unity—in which kinesthetic holding-still is [also] a mode of the "I do." Clearly the aspect-exhibitions of whatever body is appearing in perception, and the kinestheses, are not processes [simply running] alongside each other; rather, they work together in such a way that the aspects have the ontic meaning of, or the validity of, aspects of the body only through the fact that they are those aspects continually required by the kinestheses. . .[12]

This passage continues by noting that the ego itself is constituted in these acts:

> [S]ensibility, the ego's active functioning of the living body
> or the bodily organs. . . proceeds in consciousness not as a
> mere series of body-appearances, as if these in themselves,
> through themselves alone and their coalescences, were
> appearance of bodies; rather, they are such in conscious-
> ness only in combination with the kinesthetically function-
> ing living body. . .[13]

This leads Husserl to the some of the most subtle and challenging developments of his thought. He had emphasized more and more that understanding and use are basic to thought and to self-constitution. But our activity in the world is common as well as active; "[c]onstantly functioning in wakeful like, we also function together, in the manifold ways of considering, together, objects pregiven to us in common, thinking together, valuing, planning, acting together."[14]

Husserl saw our bodily nature as the key to this intersubjective quality of the world. He seems to have had this insight early in his career, though it was difficult for him to reconcile it with his desire to give phenomenology the solid grounding of the Cartesian cogito. In a brilliant and difficult set of deductions, found in the fifth Cartesian Meditation, Husserl attempted to move from the apparent solipsism of static phenomenology to the immediate experience of others. We can experience ourselves as subjects, as actors; but we are also visible to ourselves, to our sight and touch. We are simultaneously lived bodies and physical objects, and this duality brings us to a primordial, non-propositional experience of other people (and, surprisingly, other animals) as alter egos.

The experience we have is not a fusion of minds; as Husserl points out, if we knew another's thoughts as she does she would no longer be an Other. It is, instead, a sort of vector of co-participation, through which we orient and constitute each other in the cultural and temporal world we inhabit and embody. "[H]uman existence as such is always related consciously to an existent practical world as a surrounding world already endowed with humanly significant predicates" built through our common past "in human undergoing and doing."[15] This common world, moreover, itself takes its meaning from being situated within a multiplicity of worlds:

> The objective world is the psycho-physical world, and it is the cultural world that has received its cultural predicates from functioning human subjectivity bestowing them, predicates that possess their manner of experience and disclosure, but of such a manner of experience and disclosure that it presupposes the objective experience of alien subjects and their lived body/spiritual functioning.[16]

Anthony Steinbock has recently drawn out some of the implications of this strain in Husserl's thought in *Home and Beyond: Generative Phenomenology After Husserl.*

Husserl's own success in squaring this insight with his desire to create a new Cartesianism was a failure, and soon after he started revising the *Cartesian Meditations* he abandoned the work. In the last years of his life he turned toward a theory centered on concrete aspects of the human "lifeworld"—the persistent horizon of our common lives. It is "what we know best, what is always taken for granted in all human life, always familiar to us in its typology through experience."[17] "Thus in general the world exists not only for isolated men but for the community of men; and this is due to the fact that even what is straightforwardly perceptual is communalized."[18]

The concept of the lifeworld is among Husserl's most fruitful and radical concepts. It finds echoes in the work of cognitive scientists like Andy Clark, and has been given new support by recent neurological research. Our sense of ourselves and others turns out to rest on many–layered resonances, reflections and echoes in which each of us actually embodies the acts of others—not through intuition but in direct neurological mirroring.[19]

The most decisive evidence comes from the discovery of "mirror neurons" in the mid-1990s by University of Parma neurologists

Giovanni Rizzolatti, Vittorio Gallese, and others, first in monkeys and later in humans. They described the cells this way:

> The main functional characteristic of mirror neurons is that they become active both when the monkey makes a particular action (for example, when grasping an object or holding it), and when it observes another individual (monkey or human) making a similar action. Typically, mirror neurons do not respond to the sight of a hand mimicking an action in the absence of the target. Similarly, they do not respond to the observation of an object alone, even when it is of interest to the monkey.[20]

Nor do they respond when the object of interest is grasped by a tool.

A large number of different groups of mirror neurons have now been found, leading Gallese and Rizzolati to the conclusion that "action observation involves *action simulation*. . . . In other words, when we observe actions performed by other individuals our motor system 'resonates' along with that of the observed agent."[21]

This would not have been an unfamiliar idea to Husserl and his contemporaries. Edith Stein, one of the most brilliant of his students, made a similar argument in her treatment of "sentient contagion":

> [T]here's such a thing as the impact of one sentient individual upon another when no mental functioning of any kind is in play. What makes this possible is a *modification of the behavior* of one individual under the influence of another, a *conformity of behavior* of a series of individuals who mutually influence one another, and finally an *intermeshing of functionalities* of different individuals which serves *objectively* one purpose. What is *not* possible without mental activation is any *stance-taking* of the individuals to one another. . .[22]

This and other similarities suggest that Husserlian intersubjectivity makes a better fit with contemporary neuroscience than the Standard Cognitive Science Model does. For example, it provides a simpler and more convincing account of the ways through which we see others as possessing minds like our own, what in cognitive science is called the Theory of Mind.

Within the standard input/output paradigm other minds are truly Other. It is generally supposed among cognitive scientists that in order to make sense of the rest of humanity we need an unconscious or semi-conscious body of propositions about "what people are like." While a minority holds that we conduct mental simulations of others' possible acts, the mainstream sticks with the notion of quasi-linguistic rules of thumb. In the words of Steven Pinker, a vociferous proponent and popularizer of the Standard Cognitive Science Model, "Our minds . . . are fitted with mechanisms designed to read the goals of other people so we can copy their intended acts."[23]

Because of the detailed and intertwined resonances between our sensorimotor systems and those of other people and animals, though, we no longer need to assume an intervening interpretive module to account for the theory of mind. Our knowledge of others, Husserl would say, is founded in passive syntheses. This theory, as it is being developed by Vittorio Gallese and his colleagues, is different from both the propositional theory of Pinker and others and even the standard form of simulation theory. Gallese points out:

> [T]he way I characterize simulation is different from the notion of simulation discussed by the proponents of Simulation Theory. According to Simulation Theory, the pretend state used by the interpreter in order to understand the behaviour of the agent, is the result of a deliberate and voluntary act on the side of the interpreter. The simulation process I am discussing is instead *automatic, unconscious and pre-reflexive.*[24]

Mirror neurons, which Pinker does not discuss, incorporate the experience of others directly. The "shared manifold" we inhabit and embody has many layers, including conscious psychological analysis and "mind reading," but it is founded upon our neurological reflection of each other. It is in the very constitution of our world, not in any symbolic reduction and reflection upon it, that we constitute ourselves within a "correlative and reversible we-centric space."[25]

Husserl had set himself against representationalism early on; as he wrote in the Logical Investigations, "I have an idea of the god Jupiter: this means that I have a certain presentative experience, the presentation-of-the-god-Jupiter is realized in my consciousness. This intentional experience may be dismembered as one chooses in descriptive analysis, but the god Jupiter will naturally not be found in it."[26] And this had eventually led him to the insight that the ego could no longer be considered "an isolated thing alongside other such things in a pregiven world. [With phenomenology t]he serious problem of personal egos external to or alongside each other comes to an end in favor of an intimate relation of beings in each other and for each other."[27]

Rizzolatti and Gallese's work is extraordinarily important and suggestive; V.S. Ramachandran has called it "the single most important 'unreported' (or at least, unpublicized) story of the decade."[28] It lends additional weight and depth to Husserlian phenomenology and to enactivist cognitive science, and shows that some of the questions debated in rival theories are at best pseudo-problems.

It also contributes to an account of human evolution in which language itself can be seen to emerge out of preconceptual thinking and spontaneous gesture. Intriguingly, Rizzolatti and Gallese's group have found that the mirror neurons for hand gestures in monkeys are focused in the area of the cortex comparable to Broca's area, one of the major speech centers in the human brain. Speech and gesture thus share biological ties, and it may well be that one evolved from the other.

But this approach takes away as well as gives. Conventional cognitive science holds out the promise of determining the substance of human activity from neurological data or computational models. Pinker's The Blank Slate is an attempt at making good on this promise.

It presents us with a straightforward choice between sociobiological innateness and a kind of straw-man view that we are *tabulae rasae*, empty vessels waiting to be filled by environmental shaping. Since it pictures humans as independent observer/actors, choosing actions by reference to innate rules, and since it needs to explain how we manage to understand and agree with each other more times than not, its presuppositions lead almost invariably to the conclusions that we have similar or identical rulebooks and that our rules have strong, conduct-shaping content.

If our desires and behavior are innate or strongly shaped by our genetic inheritance, though, our "true nature" is essentially static; human history is too short for natural selection to have had any effect. Pinker's book is, indeed, designed to show us "the voice of the species. . . : that infuriating, endearing, mysterious, predictable, and eternally fascinating thing we call human nature."[29]

Tricked out with the latest in scientific jargon and delivering a message that "everything is the way it is *for a good reason*," Pinker gives just what a popular audience requires: a frosting of hard-headed illusion-busting over a socially conservative cake. Sociobiology, refashioned as "evolutionary psychology," does one thing well: it comes up with just-so fables that assure us that today's beliefs and institutions are the unshakable products of evolutionary wisdom. These stories are just as plausible as the coherent, rational, and useful theories of witchcraft-caused illness in some African communities, and just as likely to be wrong.

The Standard Cognitive Science Model, by reducing human activity to the expression of internalized, static, and uniform rules, casts humans as isolated actors but paradoxically treats them as identical, interchangeable units. As we are all similarly programmed, we can all be integrated into a larger body of rule-governed activities. The theory thus reproduces more than the methodological individualism with which it began; it also justifies and facilitates the type of command-oriented military organization whose interests gave rise to cognitivism in the first place.

Theories that account for the mutual interactions of organism, heredity, and environment, the "triple helix" of Pinker's bête noire Richard Lewontin, picture collective activity differently. Like the phenomenologists and scientists like Edelman, Varela, Clark, Gallese, and other critics of computationalism, they have shown a world that we constitute and recreate constantly, but which gives us no guidance except for our mutable pasts and our mutual dependence. It is a world that seems to have texture but no content. And Wittgenstein may have intuited this in the passage cited near the beginning of this essay, because he goes on to write:

> Why should the order [of language] not proceed, so to speak, out of chaos? The case would be like the following—certain kinds of plants multiply by seed, so that a seed always produces a plant of the same kind as that from which it was produced—but *nothing* in the seed corresponds to the plant which comes from it; so that it is impossible to infer the properties or structure of the plant from those of the seed that comes out of it—this can only be done from the *history* of the seed.

(This is not at all contradicted by the human genome project, which can rely only on history in an attempt to associate genes with their expression.)

We are thus returned to ourselves, as it were—back to the everyday, and back, too, to our own past. And this was the same problem Husserl had to face at the end of his life, as he continued to search for grounded and certain knowledge. For if the lifeworld is the product of continuous human activity, how can we ever experience phenomena *directly*? How can we get back, in Husserl's early battle cry, to "the things themselves"? The lifeworld, he was forced to conclude,

> is always already pregiven to us as impregnated by the precipitate of logical operations. The world is never given to us as other than the world in which we or others, whose store

of experience we take over by communication, education, and tradition, have already been logically active, in judgment and cognition.[30]

Therefore, *everything* arises within a communalized perception:

> [T]here is no experience, in the simple and primary sense of an experience of things, which, grasping a thing for the first time and bringing cognition to bear on it, does not already "know" more about the thing than is in this cognition alone.[31]

Husserl continued to believe in the possibility of an imaginative unraveling of all of history, a future phenomenology that could reach the primordial experience beneath the thought laid down in past generations. We need not follow him in this faith. But his own theories open a space in which particular histories have not only a certain grounding but a special relevance. For our lifeworld, which of course is not *the* lifeworld but one out of many possible lifeworlds, is one in which the intersubjective aspect of experience is not only difficult to understand; it is one in which that aspect is actively denied. It would be a mistake to assume this phenomenon as a given or to take it as a cultural universal. It has a past, and there are events and changes that we can look to as shaping moments in that past. It is also actively recreated and maintained by the social and economic institutions of the present.

Cognitive science and philosophy can bring us only so far. They can show us that we are nothing but what we make of ourselves, in common and in the passing of time. But that very realization leaves us with no choice but to inquire of our history—not the fictitious evolutionary history of sociobiology but the real history of real human communities. In *The Crisis of European Sciences and Transcendental Phenomenology* Husserl sketched a genealogy of the mathematization of the world, something that began as abstract method and ended by being taken for "true being." It is just one of the many overlapping trajectories that can be drawn backwards from our present. We may be limited to tentative, preliminary steps; but such histories at least allow us a certain distance from what would otherwise seem to be the plain facts of the human condition, and we may thereby find some insight into the ways in which we create and maintain our own presuppositions and into the possibilities of altering them.

Histories

4. LINGUISTIC TOTALITARIANISM

IN THE BEGINNING WAS THE WORD, says the evangelist; and Goethe's Faust was both right and wrong when he claimed that the act preceded it instead. Right, because no matter how vital its functions—interpreting bodily states, interrelating different cognitive spheres, maintaining attention toward needs and concerns that might otherwise remain diffuse and inchoate—language is only a part of our cognitive world. It depends on the larger context of subpersonal nonlinguistic cognition that we share with other animals, the pervasive, decentered corporeal thinking which is our common grounding, and which language neither realizes nor supplants. Like a colonizing army, language sets up its local competencies and its lines of communication, but it has no choice except to depend on the indigenous environment and to take its shape from the need to survive among its far more numerous hosts.

But Saint John is himself right. He is narrating a specifically Christian creation story, and in the Christian West the association of thinking with language has grown over time into an identification of one with the other. Discourse is expected to set forth the real nature and true form of experience, and experience acquires weight only when figured in words. We live under a kind of linguistic totalitarianism.

It is not that there is a specifically Christian attitude toward language—certainly not in the days of the evangelists, who were neither trained nor terribly interested in the niceties of Greek philosophy. But the Christian synthesis that grew up in the early centuries of the Common Era drew from a common stock of metaphors and tropes about the nature of human life and its relationship with the divine. These were the real intellectual underpinnings of antique culture, and their presuppositions continue to shape many of our own discussions.

For the Greeks, language and logic grew in the gap between gods and people. The dialectic between human and divine was a central theme for those Greek poets whose stature and influence in antiquity were comparable to that of the Bible in the Christian era. Pindar wrote:

> There is one race of men
> > one race of gods.
> > > Yet from one mother
> > > > we both take our breath.
> > > The difference
> > is in the allotment
> of all power,
> > for the one is nothing
> while the bronze sky exists forever,
> a sure abode.
> > And yet, somehow,
> we resemble the immortals,
> > whether in greatness of mind
> > > or nature, though we know not
> > to what measure
> day by day and in the watches of the night
> > fate has written that we should run.[1]

Gods and men were tied in a kind of zero-sum game. The gods are everything we are not, and we are correspondingly what *they* are not: we are changeable, we age and grow sick and die, but the gods are ageless and never vary. Our sight is limited; they can see everything. We are tied to the present, but they know the past and the future, vouchsafing an occasional insight into events through Zeus's daughters, the Muses. We see as through a glass, darkly. They see face to face.

Those who recognize only the magnificent physicality of Greek sculpture and conclude that the Greeks were the first to conceive and realize a humanistic art, celebrating and exalting the individual, misunderstand what the Greeks were doing. These were statues of gods, great men inspired by the gods, or athletes in the fleeting moment in which they attained godlike powers; and if in their bodies they were similar to us, these images were completely unlike those of mortals in their radiant and unchanging perfection. The Greek worshipper, sick or hungry or simply out of shape like most people, was not fooled as we are by the human form of Zeus or Apollo. The fact that men and gods shared a single physical shape only emphasized the unbridgeable gulf between them; the ideal harmony of the body of the gods presented men with a measure of the weakness and transience of human existence.

The humanity of the gods both uplifted and condemned. In the light of their presence the Greeks saw with cruel precision the inadequacies and miseries of merely human life. Their splendor measured our insignificance. Sir Kenneth Clark, in his magisterial study of the nude, gives only half the equation: the human form of the gods, as presented in Greek statuary, "takes the vague fears of the unknown and sweetens them by showing that the gods are like men and may be worshipped for their life-giving beauty rather than their death-dealing powers."[2] It surely does this, but it just as surely shows up our flabby, misshapen, failing flesh as a ludicrous parody of our ideal form.

However it is figured in art, story, or dogma, the human condition remains unsatisfactory; as Robert Frost put it in one of his most stinging poems

No memory of having starred
Atones for later disregard
Or keeps the end from being hard. ("Provide, provide")

The classical era saw any number of solutions to this insoluble problem, and the fact that the schools of the Hellenistic period have become names for character types—Epicurean, Stoic, Skeptical, Cynical—shows the perspicacity and thoroughness of their analyses. All of them offered a cure for life's sorrows. The one that concerns us here is Stoicism, and it based its power over one's character and emotional life on a comprehensive analysis of the universe.

In every European language "stoical" means "impassive," and between that definition and perhaps a reference to Marcus Aurelius we often pass on to more appealing topics like neoplatonism. But the philosophy of the Stoa was among antiquity's grandest intellectual accomplishments, one of those huge philosophical systems that have graced (or plagued) Western intellectual history.

In the light of the mischief such systems have caused, it would be good to know as much about the Stoics as possible. Unfortunately, unlike the Buddhist scholars of India, Western pagans had no Tibet to flee to in times of persecution, so our knowledge of Stoicism is crippled by the destruction of almost all its primary texts. Except for a few late works by Epictetus, Seneca, and Marcus Aurelius, which concentrate on the edifying rather than the systematic, and the highly sympathetic treatment of Stoic theories in Cicero and a few other Roman authors, little more than fragments remain. We can make out, however, a cosmology of repeated cycles of destruction and creation that coincidentally anticipates the physics of the Big Bang, a detailed analysis of logic, predication, and the functioning of signifiers and signified in language that show Stoicism to be a precursor of contemporary semiotics, and an unusual and revealing account of the emotions.

To the Stoics "all the emotions come about through judgment and opinion."[3] It is hard to imagine a theory more absurd on its face. Emotional responses seem completely separate from the deliberation we associate with opinion. But this theory arises logically from the Stoics' starting points.

Though they held that the mind at birth was a *tabula rasa*, the Stoics recognized nothing like an unmediated sense impression, the mere inscription on the mind of an image of something outside. Instead, every sense impression in a rational being was a proposition expressed in interior speech, and this proposition was accompanied by an act of assent or a kind of evaluation:

> Sensory impressions are ones obtained through one or more sense-organs, non-sensory are ones obtained through thought such as those of the incorporeals and of the other things acquired by reason. Some sensory impressions arise from what is, and are accompanied by yielding and assent. But impressions also include appearances which are quasi-products of what is. Furthermore, some impressions are rational, and others non-rational. Those of rational animals are rational, and those of non-rational animals are non-rational. Rational impressions are thought processes; irrational ones are nameless.[4]

When I look at a blank page I am not a passive recipient of whiteness. Instead, I give assent to the proposition that "before me is a white page"—not a hallucination of a white page, or a conjured-up vision of one, or even a red page rendered white by being observed under red light. (These others are appearances, and the Stoic would withhold yielding and assent from them.) For the Stoics, everything we see, hear, smell, taste, or touch becomes an internal linguistic utterance that asserts a particular state of affairs.

The building blocks of the Stoic mind are these "sayables"—*lekta*. Every sayable "is what subsists in accordance with a rational impression, and a rational impression is one in which the content of the impression can be exhibited in language."[5] Such an analysis presents an astute appreciation of how much thinking goes into the simplest of experiences. Indeed, the Stoics drew an almost Kantian distinction between those things that give rise to sense impressions and the way in which sense impressions subsist in the mind. But they did not share Kant's critical approach. On questions of knowledge they held a realist position, most holding that a true impression could be discerned from a false one by its character—though Cicero admitted that this was "the one controversial issue which has lasted" to his day.[6] The result was a general assumption that reality was spontaneously translated into discourse in an unproblematic way.

Thus the relationship between words and things was not of central importance to the Stoic project. What was crucial instead was the way their presuppositions extended language to cover the whole of existence, as Augustine observed:

> [The Stoics say that from the senses] the mind forms conceptions—*ennoiai*, as they call them—of those things, that is, which they articulate by definition. The entire method of learning and teaching, they say, stems and spreads from there.[7]

In Stoicism we find the first consistent example of the Western tendency to turn everything into language.

Their subsequent reasoning is simple. Since all mental activity is propositional, the starting point of all human activity can be nothing other than a linguistic proposition. Acts are therefore based on judgments. If I move my arm, it follows in every case that I've decided that now is an appropriate time to move my arm. If I run away in fear, I must have determined that it was proper to run and that it was proper to feel terrified. If I am angry, it is because I have concluded that under the circumstances that I perceive at the time it is appropriate for me to feel and express anger. It is in this sense that all emotions are opinions.

The Stoics did not deny that humans were subject to the sensations of the body. These, however, were specifically denied the status of thoughts. They were not to be confused with the discursive mental activity that was the true form of emotional life:

> None of the things which rouse the mind fortuitously should be called passions; the mind suffers them, so to speak, rather than causes them. Therefore, *passions consist not in being moved as a result of impressions of things, but in surrendering oneself to them*

> *and following up this fortuitous movement.* For if anyone thinks
> that pallor, floods of tears, sexual arousal, heavy breathing or
> a sudden brightening of the eyes and the like, are evidence of
> passion and a mark of the mind, he is mistaken and fails to
> realize that these are bodily drives. . . . Anger not only has to
> be moved but to rush out. This is because it is an impulse,
> and impulse never exists without the mind's assent. For it is
> impossible that any action concerning revenge and punish-
> ment should take place without the mind's awareness.[8]

It is worth noting here that although the Stoics were technically materialists, analyses such as this leave mind and body incompatible. Passions or impulses are mental phenomena and therefore propositional. They must be distinguished from bodily drives, which are fortuitous physical events, assimilated to "things" and thus in a sense external to the self.

In the Stoic view emotions arise from two connected errors of judgment. First is the mistaken belief that what has happened is of actual importance: "wild delight and desire are caused by beliefs about what is good. . . [and] fear and distress are caused by beliefs about what is bad."[9] These are almost always false beliefs, of course, such as the common fallacy that money and the pleasures of sexually attractive companions are desirable goods and poverty and death are evils to be avoided. (It was not that the Stoics were averse to pleasure or success. Apparent goods such as health, life, pleasure, beauty, wealth, and noble birth were most often classified as "preferred indifferents"—indifferent in moral value but preferred if the choice created no larger complications.)

The other error underlying emotion is the opinion that it is proper or appropriate to experience one: "when our belief in the seriousness of our misfortune is combined with the further belief that it is right, and an appropriate and proper thing, to be upset by what has happened, *then, and not before,* there comes about the deep emotion which is distress."[10]

This analysis immediately points to the cure for the "disease" of emotion. "[T]he entire theory of emotion can be summed up in a single point: that they are all in our power, all experienced through judgment, all voluntary. It is . . . error, then, that must be removed, . . . belief that has to be taken away."[11] Once the intellectual errors supporting emotional responses are brought to light and the old habits that encouraged inappropriate passions uprooted, the wise person will enter a state of serenity, no longer falling into distress or sorrow, allowing himself the "well-reasoned swelling" of joy instead of indulging in excessive gladness.[12] This is the road to what we still call a Stoic temperament.

Stoicism is often and properly seen as a form of philosophical therapy. Its "treatment modality" is putting an end to desire, and to many it thus seems to echo Buddhism's four Noble Truths: Life is suffering, suffering arises from selfish desires, these desires can be eliminated, and the Buddha's eight-fold path is the method that leads to the cessation of desire.

In some respects this is a fruitful comparison. Both the Stoic wise man and the bodhisattva experience the physical promptings of emotion but remain detached from them. Neither sage dwells on these sensations or builds narratives and conclusions about them, and without this mental machinery to amplify and prolong them the promptings come, transform, and dissipate without any power to distress or upset.

Like most such supposed cross-cultural parallels, though, this similarity cannot be pushed too far before it becomes seriously misleading. It is true that both Buddhists and Stoics aim at the extirpation of desire. But they do this in different ways. The Stoics, following a rational structure of propositions grounded in physics and psychology, trained themselves to act in accord with their conclusions. Buddhism, on the other hand—especially the philosophical schools of the Mahayana—tends toward a rejection of all such structures, and Buddhist thinkers are famously suspicious of the claims of propositional logic to grasp and express reality.

A brief comparison with the brilliant Madhyamika school of Indian Buddhism may highlight the distinctively Western aspects of the Stoic project. The Madhyamika school, beginning with the work of Nagarjuna (second or third century CE), is characterized by a relentlessly deconstructive criticism of all views—not just philosophical positions but everyday notions like causation. Nagarjuna's masterpiece, *The Fundamental Wisdom of the Middle Way*, pushes a form of negative theology to the point where it can be hard to distinguish from pure nihilism.

Nagarjuna's position, though, is no more nihilist than that of a negativist theologian like Simone Weil. Weil once said that one did not have to search for god, but simply say no to everything that is not god, and for Nagarjuna the longing for serenity that drove the Stoics was just another of the desires that needed to cease. He would have been sure, in addition, that the rationalist Stoic path was self-defeating. *The Fundamental Wisdom of the Middle Way* devotes itself to demonstrating that every attempt to grasp the world in thought founders on contradictions. It shows all reasoning to be a series of vicious circles and turns rationality on itself until all its pretensions vanish. None of our ideas about the world and no theory of existence is left standing.

Instead of objects acting on other objects and instead of real selves seeking real nirvana there is only an infinitely complex and never-ending process of mutual transformation. Everything in the universe is the product of this dependent origination and is "empty"—that is, devoid of intrinsic being. But this, too, is a philosophical position, no different from the positions of the Madhyamika's opponents, and emptiness cannot become the cornerstone of a "correct" view of the world; the Madhyamika's deconstructive process must turn on itself if it is to be either consistent or effective:

> The victorious ones have said
> That emptiness is the relinquishing of all views.
> For whomever emptiness is a view
> That one has accomplished nothing.[13]

Paradoxical as it sounds, Nagarjuna means what he says.[14] What the Madhyamika proposes is not a correct view of things that should be substituted for error; as Nagarjuna wrote, "I have no proposition and therefore I have no fallacy."[15] The conventional truth of appearances is not a delusion to dispel. It is the way in which the interconnected transformations of dependent origination necessarily appear to us, much as the earth's rotation is evident to us in the form of the apparent rising and setting of the sun. What the Madhyamika assert (or assert/negate) is that any analysis of the world or any attempt to grasp its truth is illegitimate and doomed to fail:

> Any attempt to stand outside this life and this world, in an appeal to some higher authority by virtue of which one may pronounce final judgments over conventional affairs—either "negating" them en masse, or else grounding them in a transcendental reality—is destined for continual frustration because it proceeds from a fundamental contradiction. . . . The real task is completely to surrender the compulsion to define any and every problem in the propositional structure and vocabulary of rationalism.[16]

Nagarjuna now appears in Zen genealogies as the fourteenth Indian Patriarch. There was no Zen Buddhism in his day, but this purely legendary role is a fitting one. The Zen koan owes a great deal to Madhyamika logic and plays a similarly self-destructive function. It is a problem that sounds as if it has a real but difficult-to-find solution. But the koan is in fact unanswerable. It can be "solved" only when the student realizes that all thinking plays similar tricks, leading us into endless troubles as we substitute our intellectual constructions for the life that is plainly visible all around us. Philosophical systems and visionary experiences are delusions. Everyday life is nirvana, and ordinary mind is the Buddha nature. Asked by a student what his miraculous actions were, one Zen master answered, "When I'm hungry, I eat. When I'm tired, I sleep."

This is not how the Stoic solution works at all. Stoic therapy works through the very type of intellectual structure that the Madhyamika argued was full of contradictions. It is a talking cure—perhaps the first of a long line of such practices—and its efficacy depends on the patient's accepting the truth of its propositions (as truths, of course, and not as comforting illusions) and shaping his inner life as those propositions demand. Crucially, the propositional structure ends up substituting itself for what we had taken to be reality.

In a style of advertisement common to classical philosophies, the Stoics claimed to teach "a life in agreement with and consistent with nature."[17] But theirs was an odd kind of nature. It did not come naturally. The Stoics argued that human beings were designed by nature to exercise reason, but that their other inclinations often conflicted with rational ends. It was therefore necessary to discipline oneself until one's actions were in accordance with reason. Only then was one truly living in agreement with nature:

> [S]ince reason, by way of a more perfect management, has been bestowed on rational beings, to live correctly in accordance with reason comes to be natural for them, for reason supervenes as the craftsman of impulse.[18]

The discursive second nature of Stoic theory is our real home as rational beings, even if we do not begin with an immediate apprehension that this is so. We must train ourselves to live by it—to leave our first home in the body and take up residence in the perfect truths of the mind. In time we will come to see that the "natural" of our initial experience of life is unsatisfactory when compared with the "natural" of the rational order:

> [A] man's first affiliation is with those things which are accordance with nature. But as soon as he has acquired understanding, or rather, the conception which the Stoics call *ennoia*, and has seen the regularity and, so to speak, the harmony of conduct, he comes to value this higher than all the objects of his initial affection; and he draws the rational conclusion that this

constitutes the highest human good. . . [R]ight action is not
present in the first affiliations of nature. Yet it is in accordance
with nature, and stimulates us to desire it far more strongly
than we are stimulated by all the earlier objects.[19]

There was nothing novel in this rejection of the apparently natural;
it, too, was a commonplace of antique thought. The Greeks were
inordinately proud of their way of life, but they did not see it as
something that had emerged spontaneously. Their pride arose
instead from a sense that the life of the polis was an accomplishment, virtually a work of art, and they often distinguished this civilized state from the miseries of nature.

Three centuries of Hellenophilia have left us with an erroneous
ideal of Greek naturalness. We tend to see Greek athletic nudity as
one sign of this imaginary quality. To us nakedness is a natural and
often enviable prelapsarian state, reserved for innocent children per-
mitted to play at the beach *au naturel* and advocated by fans of cloth-
ing-optional recreation who call themselves "naturists." The Greeks
thought differently. They pointed to the year in which Olympic athletes competed nude as a milestone in their rise to the civilized state.
Public nudity was a hard-won achievement, not a manifestation of a
natural way of life.

Nor would today's advocates of a "natural" diet find a welcome in
classical Greece. In the opinion of one of the Hippocratic texts
uncivilized existence is so inimical to human flourishing that even
the foods found in the wild are harmful:

> . . . in primitive times, men often suffered terribly from their
> indigestible and animal-like diet, being liable to violent pain
> and sickness and a speedy death. Certainly such ills would
> probably prove less serious than now because they were accus-
> tomed to this kind of food, but even then, such illnesses would
> have been serious and would have carried off the majority of a
> weak constitution although the stronger would survive longer.

...For this reason I believe these primitive men sought food
suitable for their constitution and discovered that which we
now use. Thus, they took wheat and wetted it, winnowed it,
ground it, sifted it, and then mixed it and baked it into bread,
and likewise made cakes from barley. They boiled and baked
and mixed and diluted the strong raw foods with the weaker
ones and subjected them to many other processes, always with
a view to man's nature and his capabilities.[20]

We need to keep in mind the extreme artificiality (in no derogatory
sense) and fragility of civilization in the classical mind. The elite of the
time would not find the discipline demanded by Stoicism at all unusual.

In the practice of antiquity, in fact, Stoicism was only one among
many schools that proposed to guide the project of crafting a life.
The aristocratic warriors of the *Iliad* risked and often embraced
death in order to leave behind a good name; indeed, Achilles explicitly chooses death:

If I hold out here and I lay siege to Troy,
My journey home is gone, but my glory never dies.
If I voyage back to the fatherland I love,
my pride, my glory dies. . .
true, but the life that's left me will be long,
the stroke of death will not come on me quickly.[21]

Turned toward the common good in the rituals of the *poleis*, transformed into cults of salvation and improvised by working-class sodali-
ties in the Hellenistic cities, the ideal life in antiquity remained one that
was consciously shaped and directed toward some end. As everyone
knew, neither the unexamined nor the unshaped life was worth living.

What was distinctive about the Stoic project, instead, was the way
it constructed and then operated within a linguistic model of the
world. Unlike the Epicureans, who were said to have rejected dialectic, the Stoics devoted much energy and time to the analysis of

propositions and logical fallacies. The great Stoic logician Chrysippus wrote dozens of books on topics such as ambiguity, the "lying argument," the "veiled argument," the "not-someone argument" and so on; like everything else he wrote, these are lost. This attention to logic was no doubt a defensive measure. The therapeutic claims made by Stoicism and its followers' willingness to undergo its mental discipline were dependent on the validity of Stoic reasoning and on the accuracy of its starting points. If they could not translate the entire world into language, they lost their authority.

And the universalization of discourse proposed by the Stoics opened up another possibility: the world as project. The self-control justified by the correctness of the Stoic system could slip easily into exercising control over others, because that same system had the potential for subjecting everything to its judgment. As every small child discovers, language is a tool of power. To assert that language can grasp all of reality is to claim power over everything.

But though Stoicism was understandably popular among the rulers of the Roman empire, the possibility of turning its methodology toward reconstructing the world itself remained unexplored. This is not surprising, because it was content to duplicate or explicate the world. It had no starting point outside of it, and in this it was much more integrated into the classical mainstream than was Platonism.

In general, classical philosophies fell into one of two categories. Rationalists like the Stoics tended to see the divine as immanent rather than transcendent. Though the Stoic universe was rational, it rendered the gods into the same structure as everything else. God was fully immanent in creation, as Cicero explains:

> [Chrysippus] says that divine power resides in reason and in the mind and intellect of universal nature. He says that god is the world itself, and the universal pervasiveness of mind; also that he is the world's own commanding-faculty, since he is located in intellect and reason; that he is the common nature of things, universal and all-embracing; also the force of fate

LINGUISTIC TOTALITARIANISM

> and the necessity of future events. In addition he is fire; and
> the aether of which I spoke earlier; also things in a natural
> state of flux and mobility, like water, earth, air, sun, moon
> and stars; and the all-embracing whole; and even those men
> who have attained immortality.[22]

Beautiful as this is, it leaves god nowhere as well as everywhere. If the cosmos was amenable to elucidation, it was also without direction.

The alternative was a providentialist outlook, which preserved the freedom of the pagan gods but left their purposes inscrutable. Many writers treated both as reasonable possibilities, and none was able to construct another alternative so long as the guiding metaphor remained a "common city of gods and men."

It took Christianity to create and propagate a model at once rational and purposeful. The god of Christianity is transcendent, of course, and unlike the pagan gods even at their most powerful he directs history as a whole instead of locally and in detail rather than in generalities. In addition, his overarching purposes are rationally explicable. Thus, the proper combination of reason and revelation will spell out the truth of all things.

Stoicism had no immediate future in the Christian world. It was not overtly atheistic like Epicureanism, but its cosmology of endless recurrence was incompatible with Genesis, its theories of perception and truth were irrelevant, and its ethics seemed repellent in an age where the all-consuming love of God was the touchstone of virtue.

What survived, whether consciously or not, was its ambition to embrace the whole of the cosmos in discourse elaborated from natural principles, an ambition that was revived in Early Modern philosophy. The Stoic project is the archetype of Cartesian rationalism and its successors and critics through Hegel and Marx. Wittgenstein thought he had demolished the pretensions of systematic philosophy in the *Tractatus*, making the grandly self-mocking boast that he had solved all the problems that philosophy could solve and had simultaneously shown how little was accomplished by doing this.

He succeeded to the extent of putting an effective end to system-spinning in philosophy. But the lure of perfect rational knowledge has proved too great.

Linguistic totalitarianism survived. It has become almost impossible for us to conceive of anything outside discourse. Ethicists continue to build chains of argument to ground right conduct in contract, the original state behind the veil of ignorance or the virtues or a utilitarian calculus, as if the only problem with philosophy is that it hasn't been tried hard enough. Wittgenstein's almost Zen-like pointing to the unwritten half of the *Tractatus*—the most important part, he insisted—was ignored completely; it was as if he had written, "what cannot be said clearly can be safely ignored." We read that the postmodern world is one of incompatible language games, which in truth is no different from any other kind of world; but postmodernists can conceive of nothing outside of language and its games, which now float in the void like galaxies instead of surfacing above the waves of subpersonal cognition like a chain of islands.

These are only annoyances. Far worse is the way the pretensions of language have become an obstacle to human life. People have always died for religion, but only with the triumph of the linguistic have they begun dying for philosophy. The certainty that a rational system could judge the world became a warrant for real totalitarianism.

The modern era is littered with attempts to subject people and communities to disciplines far more cruel than any a Stoic might impose upon himself. More horrible yet, they were justified by truth and virtue: Robespierre and the Terror, carried out in the name of the French people and of Reason; the Leninist certainty that history was a science and that a vanguard party could push Russia to communist utopia; the slaughter of the Jews in the name of a theory of race; and the slaughter of Cambodians in the name of agrarian equality: all were justified by logically elaborated propositions that explained how the world worked, what was wrong with it and how it could be improved. SS men might have been revolted at the sight of another Jewish child being forced into the gas chamber, but Himmler could console them with the argument that their unpleasant duty would clear the way to a bright future. A U.S. Secretary of State, asked about the deaths of Iraqi children caused by the sanctions her government insisted upon, said that this was an acceptable price to pay for her policy goals. Hundreds and thousands die annually as a by-product of "reforms" that will, the IMF assures us, benefit their survivors—assuming they leave any. The Athenians did not bother to justify their slaughter of the Melians; it was always the rule, they said, that "the strong do what they can and the weak suffer what they must."[23] These days the Melians would end up just as dead, but we would assure them in advance that ours was the only right course of action.

There are kinder, gentler forms of linguistic totalitarianism, too. Margaret Thatcher put forth neoliberalism as the one conceivable social system, summarizing her argument as TINA—There Is No Alternative. The administration of George W. Bush is addicted to this, in its incessant appeal to universals running from the relatively unexceptional to the outrageous:

> People everywhere want to say what they think; choose who will govern them; worship as they please; educate their children—male and female; own property; and enjoy the benefits of their labor. These values of freedom are right and true for every person, in every society—and the duty of protecting these values against their enemies is the common calling of freedom-loving people across the globe and across the ages. . . . Policies that further strengthen market incentives and market institutions are relevant for all economies—industrialized countries, emerging markets, and the developing world.[24]

On what is usually taken to be the other end of the American political spectrum, the individualist leftism of Noam Chomsky, there is the same refusal to see the complexity of real human interactions and a leaning toward naïve realism, the belief that what we encounter outside us are the facts, which we can render into words transparently.

This bias seems to arise from Chomsky's linguistic theory, since it is also found in his more conservative followers like Steven Pinker.

Language always conceals the wordless thought from which it begins, thought that belies language's claims. Beneath its spurious universality and the discrete language-games of the postmodernist vision lies our common grounding in the life of the body, always changing and different in unpredictable ways in different times and communities. It is not that we lack a foundation for understanding; but our common foundation is, as Mendelssohn said of music, too concrete to be put into words. The great Russian psychologist Lev Semyonovich Vygotsky wrote,

> If the thoughts of two people coincide, perfect understanding can be achieved through the use of mere predicates, but if they are thinking about different things they are bound to misunderstand each other. . . .As Tolstoy noted, those who are accustomed to solitary, independent thinking do not easily grasp another's thoughts and are very partial to their own; but people in close contact apprehend one another's complicated meanings by "laconic and clear" communication in the fewest words.[25]

Those common thoughts, though, are not in the form of inner speech, as both Vygotsky and the Stoics thought; they are the thoughts of the body, out of which islands of both inner and overt speech arise. Language games overlap and separate, words dance and play in the air between us. In a subtle ballet of word and glance and touch we sound harmonies and discords that resonate in speaker and hearer alike, transforming everything. In The Savage Mind Lévi-Strauss quotes an Osage: "We do not believe that our ancestors were really animals, birds, [and so on]. These things are only symbols of something higher." Which is not a bad account of language in any of its forms.

5. MONOTHEISM, MEANING, AND CERTAINTY

THE MONOTHEISTIC RELIGIONS all claim to communicate and institutionalize the truth. It is usually recognized that this was a novelty in the ancient world; what is less often noticed is how much was entailed by this assertion. In the late Roman Empire Christianity promised not truths but the Truth, not an isolated revelation of divine will but a world in which all things could be known. No mere dethroning of one paternal deity by another could accomplish this change. It was effected through a new confidence in the relationship between intellectual activity and the world, one that remains central to our concept of knowledge and our construction of self.

Of all the major monotheistic religions, Christianity is the most bound up with a specific interpretation of history. God's will is revealed not in a book but in a person, in both Jesus' words and the events of his life. The Christian message is, preeminently, that god has acted in history in specific ways and continues to govern everything that happens; as Jesus says in Luke, "Are not five sparrows sold for two farthings, and not one of them is forgotten before God? But even the very hairs of your head are all numbered."[1]

To accept this message is to find the world permeated with meaning. But the price for rendering the world a knowable whole is a split between the actual and the rational. A pattern for life was peeled off from the flux of living itself, and living achieved reality only insofar as it instantiated that pattern.

In a religious age the gap between real and actual was not a problem. So long as our inquiries began with revealed truth we had god's guarantee that our finite constructions corresponded to the true structure of a protean actuality. But he was the sole guarantor. As long as his word seemed bankable this split was tolerable. Once it was questioned, however, the problem of correspondence could no longer be avoided; but it could not be solved, either, since it was inherent in the very structure of knowledge that gave rise to it.

This remains our way of thinking, whether we are believers or consider ourselves hard-nosed rationalists. We fail to see that even our secular ways of generating and assessing explanations rest on an unprovable congruence between what is and what we can formulate. Like children given a fossil hunter's kit in a box, assured in advance that its sands contain a genuine dinosaur bone, we expect a knowable order to lie outside our thoughts, and act as if a benevolent deity had endowed us with all the tools needed to discover his plan.

The classical gods could give no such gift. They were part of the natural texture of things. Fellow-players in a game of infinite complexity who acted to enforce a rough moral equilibrium and saw to the well-being of those cities that maintained their ritual obligations, they neither structured nor guided the world. Everything was potentially subject to their influence, but they were equally likely to leave humanity to its own devices. This is as true of the intellectualized deities of later antiquity as it was for Homer's pantheon. Plutarch says

> it is difficult to define precisely how and to what extent providence should be invoked, both those who deny that god is responsible for everything, and those who make him responsible for practically everything, alike fail to achieve a reasonable and appropriate solution.[2]

It is hard to find classical exponents of a truly universal providential order. The Stoics are said to be providentialists, but many held that the divine intent "pervades some parts to a greater extent and others to a lesser degree;" the Stoic Cleanthes's hymn to Zeus ends in a bathetic fall: "no deed is done on earth, god, without your offices, nor in the divine ethereal vault of heaven, nor at sea, save what bad men do in their folly."3

Chance—tyche—continued to rule history and individual life, and its vagaries formed part of the appeal of history:

> Since the issue depends on fortune, while the motivation and execution do not, it is in these that the student can perceive the struggle of virtue with circumstance, or the play of intelligent daring in the face of danger, when reason joins forces with the emotions of the moment.4

A history built on the interplay of character and fortune, reason, and emotion, is essentially moored in place; and from this we draw the sense, only partially misleading, that classical writers saw their world as static.

This sporadic divine involvement produced only a localized coherence. It could neither be extended from case to case nor woven into a teleological account. Herodotus, for example, explains the triumph of the Greeks over the Persian empire by the superior fighting ability of free men. But he does not suggest that this victory was inevitable or an incident in a larger history of liberty. Nor does Plutarch in his Parallel Lives. And nowhere in Plutarch's moving letter to his wife on the death of their daughter Timoxena is there any hint that her brief life was part of some divine plan.

Not that the gods were absent. The wise were always seeking insight into their intentions. But this was a difficult and uncertain task; as Heraclitus wrote, "the lord whose oracle is at Delphi neither declares nor conceals, but gives a sign."5 The intellectual sea in which the people of antiquity swam was multivalent, provisional, made up of human institutions and traditions openly admitted to be contingent. The Greeks preferred their world to all the others, of course; but Herodotus shows us with admirable evenhandedness that any number of civilizations are possible and any number of ideals of conduct are defensible.

Tolerance like Herodotus's depended on the absence of a fixed model for human behavior. Closely linked to this tolerance was an acceptance of the multiplicity of explanations that could be given for any event. If the gods were in theory subject to reason, theirs was a rationality that outstripped human understanding; all we could discern were fragments of their more comprehensive grasp, leaving us to guess at their purposes. As Lyotard puts it:

> JFL: . . .This is paganism. One does not know whom one is speaking to; one must be very prudent; one must negotiate; one must ruse; and one must be on the lookout when one has won.
>
> JLT: Because there is no outside.
>
> JFL: Right, there is no outside; there is no place from which one could photograph the whole thing.[6]

The absence of an "outside" in conventional paganism helps explain the rapid rise of the late antique cult of Mithra. David Ulansey has argued that the discovery of the precession of the equinoxes inspired this popular cult, because it suggested that the entire cosmic sphere was being rotated; and who could be capable of such a feat except a god greater than the universe itself? Because Mithra stood outside the cosmos and moved it in the immense cycle of the equinoxes, he was clearly superior to the other gods. Ulansey's hypothesis explains Mithraism's power to compete with Christianity; unlike the Olympian deities, Mithra was a genuinely transcendent pagan god, a figure who, like Yahweh, presided over everything, "the spacious firmament on high / and all the blue ethereal sky."

But the devotees of Mithra remained a minority. The enclosed and provisional cosmos of mainstream classical thought was comfortable enough for the educated and illiterate alike. The elite took pleasure in posing one explanation against another, as can be seen in Plutarch's *Table Talk*, and a particularly elegant one was greatly admired. But their luxuriant disputations were rarely ended by the unveiling of truth itself, which would have spoiled the fun. When Plutarch wants to end a dialogue with a turn toward deeper thoughts he doesn't name the winning argument. He composes a myth.

It may seem like laziness to set out contradictory accounts linked by phrases such as, "it is also said that. . ." But the pagan suspension of judgment was not a sign of a defective methodology. It rested instead on a deeply grounded appreciation of the limits of human knowledge, as modest in its pretensions to historical certainty as it was to insight into the lives of individuals. The novelist Heliodorus could easily have given a single account for the death of a character, but apparently thought it more convincing to suggest two different ones:

> [P]ossibly his enormous joy had caused the muscles of his respiratory tract to become excessively dilated and flaccid consequent upon the sudden exhaustion of his aged body; or else perhaps he had prayed for death, and the gods had granted his prayer.[7]

This is a theme we find at the very dawn of classical culture. The relativism of the sophists simply made explicit what all serious thinkers acknowledged: human understanding was weak, and absolute truth was available only in the glimpses granted through art or religion.

Not that there was much difference between these activities. Before the daunting task of naming the ships that came to Troy, Homer pauses:

> Sing to me now, you Muses who hold the halls of Olympus!
> You are goddesses, you are everywhere, you know all things—
> all we hear is the distant ring of glory, we know nothing—
> Who were the captains of Achaea? Who were the kings?[8]

Homer's extraordinary and inimitable power of presence—his ability to make people and things all but appear before us—fulfills a religious function as much as it does an artistic one. With the aid of the gods he shows us not accounts of an event but the true event itself. Without their help, in the everyday world of discourse, the perfection of divine knowledge was denied us. Tradition, reasoned debate, and the collective wisdom of the citizen body, exemplified in the councils prominent in the opening of both the *Iliad* and the *Odyssey*, were only an acceptable second–best. They helped us muddle through but never produced certainty.

The tragedies of Aeschylus and Sophocles hint at the tension between these two sorts of truth and the rich religious experience it supported. But tragedy's moment was brief. Jean-Pierre Vernant and Pierre Vidal-Naquet have argued that the form could not survive the increasing rationalization of the Greek world. To put this another way, an increasing acceptance of the quotidian and the admittedly second-best routine of civic life effectively neutralized the disruptive character of divine truth. Whatever the explanation, though, it is unlikely that any community could ever embody the profound but difficult religious realism of Sophocles. The religious life of the Hellenistic cities instead embraced a civic model of the universe in which gods and men were fellow members of a universal community: "a common city of gods and men," as Plutarch and others put it, "living together in concord and happiness with justice and virtue."[9]

In the ideology of the Hellenistic community "the greatest and most common benefit" was the divine gift of

> making [the human] race immortal through succession, by means of health bringing about marriage and the begetting of children and the procurement of the arts of nourishment.[10]

One was consoled for life's sorrows with participation in the cycles of nature and one's community and with the company of the gods themselves.

Religious life centered on the family line and the gods who founded and guarded the city. Municipal traditions and the debates in the assembly and law courts gave sufficient guidance for everyday life and a rich grounding for experiences of greater intensity. It made little difference that after the Macedonian conquest few cities in the classical Mediterranean were self-governing; the civic community remained surprisingly strong both as reality and ideal well into the fourth century C.E., and in the eastern Empire it survived even later.

Most classical religious aspiration was directed to friendship with the gods. Few acts bind a community more tightly than eating together, and in classical religion the gods shared every meal where meat was served and every cup of wine. They were present in their statues and shrines, too, and after fasting and purification the pious would consult the oracles or sleep in temples in the hope of a personal revelation. The appeal of even the mystery cults appears to have been as much intimacy with the presiding deity as it was the promise of a happy afterlife.

For many that intimacy was enough. Here is Aelius Aristides's description of a visitation by his patron deity Asclepius:

> I seemed almost to touch him and to perceive that he himself was coming, and to be halfway between sleep and waking and to want to get the power of vision and to be anxious lest he depart beforehand, and to have turned my ears to listen, sometimes as in a dream, sometimes as in a waking vision, and my hair was standing on end and tears of joy [came forth], and the weight of knowledge was no burden—what man could even set these things forth in words? But if he is one of the initiates, then he knows and understands. [11]

After such a revelation there is little need for a rational grasp of some universal plan. It is enough to know with perfect security that you are a beloved companion of a god.

For the Christians, though, mere presence was insufficient. Christianity asserted an explanation, a true understanding of the everyday as well as the exceptional; all human life was now seen under the aegis of the god of history. This required what other Hellenistic thinkers had not brought about, a split between the temporal realm of the events themselves and the perpetually valid sphere of the rational.

As Wittgenstein said, "The sense of the world must lie outside the world."[12] If events are to have significance they must be transformed into signs of something else, as the etymology suggests. But there has to be some other order of things to which the signs refer. Like Mithra, the gods of monotheism must be outside the world in order to move it and to give it structure and meaning. The intelligence that guides—indeed, dictates—events cannot be a part of those events without losing its absolute power.

Christianity is not necessarily "otherworldly" because of any hostility to the physical world or because it locates the rewards for righteousness in an afterlife. Recent work by Peter Brown and Caroline Walker Bynum has shown how closely tied early and mediaeval Christian thought was to the body. Instead, Christian thinking is otherworldly because its explanatory structure demands the existence of another world to give this one significance.

The Christian god also provides something else. There are revelations covering the stock issue for Joseph Smith's hotel in Nauvoo, Illinois, but since god generally chooses not to get bogged down in guiding every moment of everyone else's life he decided to provide us with a heuristic, a program of investigation and decision making that would yield truthful results from a truthful starting point.

Reason, a shibboleth for centuries, is not enough in itself. Meaning is reductionist; an explanation coextensive with the facts it explains is as useless as a map on a one-to-one scale. We need a criterion for selecting the truly significant aspects of any process, and that is not easily done. How can we be sure that we have separated the essential wheat from the accidental chaff? More fundamentally, how can we justify the confidence that some comprehensible system exists that can successfully model the complexity of things?

To meet this need the Christian vision also provides a vocabulary of acts, a system for identifying what truly counts in the flood of experience that passes around and through us. The revealed ordering of the cosmos was held to be the true structure of all earthly events, and its reflections on earth pointed accurately to the underlying processes of life and history. Christian explanations would thus be absolutely true. Starting with the revealed essences of events and following reason, they would trace the real armature within the confusion of mere appearance.

Christianity could thus guarantee that the world was knowable through human inquiry. It should hardly be necessary to add that even for believers the Christian explanation is almost as hopelessly complicated as the events it purports to describe. But confidence that such a explanation exists has survived its theological parentage. Its staying power derives, in part, from the surprising alliance between Christianity and pagan philosophy.

Christianity emerged within a Hellenistic world, but its intellectual structure drew very little on the philosophical schools patronized by the pagan elites. Instead, through successive "crises of self-identification" (in R.A. Markus's phrase) Christian theologians moved away from the civic, quasi-therapeutic philosophies of Stoicism and even neoplatonism to rediscover the radically anti-civic nature of Plato's thought. (It should be added that this is most accurate with respect to the Latin West; in the East, where there was far more continuity between pre-Christian and Christian cultures, neoplatonic ideas remained important.)

We often forget that philosophy was a minority pursuit in the classical world and that Plato stands furthest from the mainstream. Greek orators quoted Homer, the tragic poets, Hesiod, Pindar, or Solon; they were no more likely to cite Plato than today's legislators are to refer to Wittgenstein. There were good reasons for this. Plato's philosophy developed as a critique of the civic community. His experience under the short-lived oligarchy of the Thirty was almost as bad as that under the revived democracy, which had executed Socrates, and he had concluded that

> there will be no cessation of evils for the sons of men till either
> those who are pursuing a right and true philosophy receive
> sovereign power in the States or those in power in the States by
> some dispensation of providence become true philosophers.[13]

The solution he was to propose in the *Republic* bore no resemblance at all to the open-ended processes of Greek civic life.

Plato also attacked the quasi-religious role of Homer and the poets' claim to bring the truth of events before their audiences. Centuries of familiarity and social change had done little to diminish the intensity of the epic experience; the rhapsode Ion, in Plato's dialogue of that name, sees his audience "weeping, casting terrible glances, stricken with amazement at the deeds recounted."[14] It was through such involvement that the poets were thought to communicate the event itself rather than a mere report. But in Book X of the *Republic* Socrates hammers away at the notion that Homer possesses or communicates any knowledge, insisting that poetry presents only imitation—*mimesis*—and "has no serious claim to be valued as an apprehension of truth."[15]

Plato's greatest novelty was the redefinition of understanding as something private, discovered through introspection and reasoning. To cite only one of many versions:

> [W]hen reason . . . is hovering around the sensible world and
> when the circle of the diverse also moving truly imparts the
> intimations of sense to the whole soul, then arise opinions and
> beliefs sure and certain. But when reason is concerned with the
> rational, and the circle of the same moving smoothly declares
> it, then intelligence and knowledge are necessarily achieved.
> And if anyone affirms that in which these two are found to be
> other than the soul, he will say the opposite of the truth.[16]

By placing access to true knowledge within the individual Plato created a standpoint from which the civic world could be criticized; but since this source of knowledge was cut off from the *polis* and exempt from the vicissitudes of history, it stood to one side of everyday civic discourse. Tellingly, the version of Platonism that was influential in Cicero's and Plutarch's circles was the moderate skepticism of the later Academy, a school that to us seems Platonic only in name.

The combination of a reinvigorated Platonism with Christianity, though, created the intellectual basis for a rejection of the civic world and its replacement by a Christian commonwealth. As Peter Brown showed in *The Body and Society*, early Christian asceticism was inseparable from a desire to eliminate the ties of civic obligation, expressed most vividly in the duty to bear children for the community. Instead of the network that bound fellow-citizens to each other, their patrons, ancestors, and descendants and to the hierarchies of officials and deities, the Christian was to live in a space newly cleared of all obligations but one: his duty to god. The church found the civil community useful, but its attitude was "mingled with a spirit of inner detachment and independence, since, after all, these things belong to a perishing world and are everywhere steeped in paganism."[17] The community has played this secondary role in all subsequent western thought.

Christians lived in a far emptier world than that of pagan antiquity, but they were much more sure of themselves—a point made as much by Augustine's tone as by his logic:

> As for that characteristic which Varro produces as the distinctive mark of the New Academy, the view that everything is uncertain, the City of God roundly condemns such doubt as being madness. In matters apprehended by the mind and the reason it has most certain knowledge, even if that knowledge is of small extent on account of the "corruptible body which weighs down the mind"—as the apostle says, "Our knowledge is partial." It also trusts the evidence of the senses in every matter; for the mind employs the senses through the agency of the body, and anyone who supposes that they can never be trusted is woefully mistaken. It believes also in the

holy Scriptures, the old and the new, whence is derived the
faith which is the basis of the just man's life, the faith by
which we walk on our way without doubting, in the time of
our pilgrimage, in exile from the Lord.[18]

Augustine, though, was boasting an advantage that pagans had been
able to do without. Within the civic world one could tolerate the
absence of certain knowledge because one's life was part of a complex fabric dignified by history and ordained by the city's divine
patron. Resort to tradition by men like Cicero was thus neither an
intellectual evasion nor a sop to social conservatism; it reflected,
instead, the sense that personality and character are shaped within,
draw support from, and continually reweave the fabric of life that
preceded, surrounds, and succeeds us.

   Christianity denied the legitimacy of the tradition along with the
divinities that inspired and protected it. In return it offered an integrated structure of significance and certainty. In essence, Christianity substituted a comprehensive intellectual explanation for the
equally comprehensive lived experience of the classical city. It
opposed the truth sent from above to the facts of social life. The
most telling image of this new ideal is the Christian virgin,
metaphorically a walled garden—separated from the dialogic self-
constitution of individuals and cut off from social life, which were
now important only as they eased or blocked her path toward god.

   There is a parallel here with the almost superhuman status
claimed by the emperors from Diocletian onward, who unlike their
predecessors were exalted above their subjects like gods on earth
and whose authority was theoretically absolute and direct. This raises an important and highly charged question. Was there a hunger for
such certainty in late antique culture?

   A historiography based on Christian or post-Christian assumptions has often painted Christianity as a response to a late antique
crisis; E.R. Dodds's *Pagan and Christian in an Age of Anxiety* is a well-
known example. But the evidence for such a crisis is scattered at

best. Public life in the Empire was slowly vanishing, especially in the West, due in part to military necessity and to the autocratic rule of the fourth- and fifth-century emperors; but with the exception of Diocletian and Julian these emperors were all Christians, so this proves little. Within the earlier antique milieu much of the Christian message would have made little sense; second-century Romans admired the Christians' social virtues but were baffled by their theology and refusal to engage in debate. The calm certainty of a martyr like Perpetua was incomprehensible to her pagan father, who saw it as pride or suicidal obstinacy—terms that come up regularly in Roman accounts of Christian martyrs:

> "Daughter . . . have pity on my grey head—have pity on your father . . . if I have favored you above all your brothers, if I have raised you to reach this prime of your life. Do not abandon me to the reproach of men. Give up your pride! You will destroy all of us! None of us will ever be able to speak freely again if anything happens to you!"
>
> That was the way my father spoke out of love for me, kissing my hands and throwing himself down before me. With tears in his eyes he no longer addressed me as his daughter but as a woman. . . . I tried to comfort him saying, "It will all happen in the prisoner's dock as God wills; for you may be sure that we are not left to ourselves but are all in his power."
>
> And he left me in great sorrow.[19]

It is hard to make out the case that the population of the Empire in the first four centuries C.E. was seeking Perpetua's kind of conviction, even if it did not come at the cost of one's life.

The conversion of the Empire can be explained by more mundane factors. When Constantine legalized Christianity no more than 10 percent of the population was Christian. After Constantine only one pagan emperor took the throne; imperial funds flowed into church treasuries, pagan temples were cut off from state support and bequests to them made illegal, non-Christian schools were closed and pagan teachers barred from teaching, jobs were given preferentially to Christians, and in more than an insignificant number of cases mob violence was employed to root out obdurate pagan elements. The sum of these incentives—and there were many more—seems like an adequate explanation for the conversion of most of the Empire's population. Instead of assuming a general social malaise to which Christianity offered a cure, it is better to see Christianization as a process that exploited tensions in mainstream antique culture, seized the institutional opportunities implicit in the new political order of the post–Diocletian empire, and built a successful alternative upon elements of the minority philosophical traditions as well as the novel idea of a deity who was author of history at every level.

As above, so below. The new unity of the divine world was mirrored by a new construction of the personality, as a single, consciously knowable entity fundamentally removed from the life of the community. This new self was strikingly different from the tempered mixture of rational and emotional elements that defined the classical self-as-project and even from the functionally decentered rationalism of the Stoics, defined most of all by the rational order of fate. The god enthroned above the world called for a soul enthroned within the person, as much an absolute monarch as the Emperor in Constantinople.

Here, perhaps, is the most profound consequence of the Christianization of Europe. We continue to identify ourselves with the structure we discern in our conscious activity. The contemporary assumptions that our mental activity (conscious or not) is of a sort, which can all be brought to awareness, that it interposes between stimulus and response, forms a unified whole and can be meaningfully understood in isolation from others, all reflect the Christian picture of the soul. That picture has become self-evident. Even those who have rejected all overt theism remain bound to it. God may be dead, but the atheists keep on creating man in his image.

As recent research in the cognitive sciences shows, though, the image is deeply misleading. We imagine our conscious thinking to be something like a legislature; instead it is more like our newspaper, reporting on decisions made elsewhere, and if anything is even less reliable. The business of living is accomplished by a variety of embodied subpersonal action/perception complexes that link us with others in networks of mutual transformation, and which ask for and receive little input from conscious thought. The polymorphous complexity of Homer's heroes, self-contradictory and open to the promptings of gods, looks more accurate than the focused inwardness of Augustine.

We think we can abstract from historical and social rootedness and grasp the truth of events, mental events included. The result is that we are encouraged to live within models of experience instead of experience itself. But if they do not describe the outline of a divine order instantiated in this one, our models rest on no foundation at all. There is nothing inherent in either reason or the world that would justify their congruence, especially when we take into account the absence of criteria for deciding what to count as relevant and what to ignore. The correspondence problem of knowledge and the gap between theory and practice are not inevitable dichotomies of existence, but products of a particular explanatory system. Descartes saw this clearly, and rested his solution to the problem on his faith that a benevolent god would not allow the creatures whom he loved to fall into irremediable error. Other proposed answers have not been much more persuasive.

We may have no substitute for reason; but the problem with reason is not its instrumental value but the delusion that it can yield certainty. If that belief has encouraged free thought and radical critique, it has also furnished the justification for tyranny and terror, not least when we attempt to force others' lives into the mold of our ideals.

The assurance that we can know the truth of things was a major if not the primary support for the mathematically based scientific world view. The self-confidence that assurance inspired may have been a strategic advantage in the confrontations between the West and other cultures with less arrogant views of human powers, though European weapons were often equally effective against equally monotheistic Moslems. It should be clear by now, though, that belief that one possesses the truth can accompany the most ill-conceived ventures and all manner of atrocity.

The hijackers of September 11 could not have justified their acts as easily without the assurance that they were executing god's will. The astonishingly schematic program of conquest and reorganization in the Middle East advanced by the Project for a New American Century is not overtly religious in motivation—however George W. Bush may see it—but it depends just as much on the conviction that its proponents have an incontrovertible grasp of reality.

And the political dangers of certainty are paralleled by the impoverishment of our personal lives, for our self-identification with a supposed unified consciousness has turned us away from the dialogic complexity of human life, something that had once been reflected in the organic ideology of the ancient city. The yawning chasm we feel between self and world is an artifact of Christianization, as convincing as it is unreal—for behind it the incessant transformations of our lives continue unseen. Belief that one knows the truth is dangerous, and possession of the truth is small comfort; and in the end it turns out that the truth isn't even the truth. It is long past the time when we should have recognized that our claim to possess it expired with the literal belief in the doctrines of Christianity.

6. THE ETHICS OF WHAT AND THE ETHICS OF HOW

HOW TO GROUND ETHICS is a perennial problem. It is not made any easier by the fact that many people don't see it as a problem at all. Most of the time we have a clear idea of what's proper to do and what isn't: lying is generally frowned upon, theft is bad, killing is worse, causing pain to others should be avoided. If we press people for the reasons behind these beliefs they usually say that they are matters of common sense. Some acts just seem wrong, and we wouldn't care to spend any time with people who didn't think so. This is enough for most people. It is not, of course, enough for theorists of ethics.

Nor should it be. The unexamined ethical life runs into its own problems. It can leave us stumped in those moments of decision making that are stressed by most modern ethicists and it can blind us to the way a few small acts or a moment in which we turn away from someone or something can set us on a course that we look back on later with regret or even horror.

So where can ethical theory put its feet down? Are there some touchstones from which we can critique our decisions and those of our neighbors, or are we condemned to complete relativism, in which the Aztec farming of children for human sacrifice is as ethically neutral as eating unleavened bread at a Passover Seder? For the

Aztecs, it should be remembered, the existence of gods with an appetite for the flesh of children was a fact, and so were the benefits derived from child sacrifice and from the horror and sorrow of the people who participated—those who remembered the practice told the Franciscan Bernardino de Sahagún, "There was much compassion. They made one weep; they loosed one's weeping, they made one sad for them, there was singing for them."[1] An Aztec ethicist could justify this atrocity as a regrettable necessity, just as the Romans explained gladiatorial combat as both religious ritual and socially necessary psychodrama.

Complete relativism is unappealing and ultimately incoherent, and even most relativists differentiate between cultural practices and core moral issues where they too expect people to respond in the same way. So the question remains: how can we explain, justify, and critique these responses?

There are at least two different ways of doing this. The first starts by deciding what human beings are or should be or what place we occupy in the scheme of things. It derives principles of conduct from these conclusions. This is the ethics of what, and it characterizes most ethical thinking in the West.

The Western ethicist therefore needs a representation of the world accurate enough to work through these questions. But every model runs into the correspondence problem: it may be elegant and persuasive, but does it really explain the events in the world outside? Strictly speaking the answer to this question is always no. No rational system can lay claim to absolute truth or can be applied unproblematically. Our faith that reason can deliver certainty seems to have started with the late antique synthesis of Platonism and Christianity, and it has become such an integral part of the way we orient ourselves that we may no longer see how it had been justified in the first place and how that justification no longer holds up. But because of this problem the ethics of what runs into difficulties very quickly.

Take utilitarianism, for example, which of all ethical schools is the most likely to deny having a theory at all. Its founder was the epitome of the bluff commonsense Englishman, Jeremy Bentham, and his presupposition was that human beings, like all other animals, are machines that seek pleasure and shun pain. This very minimalist model is the ultimate justification for his famous dictum that the right thing to do is whatever produces the greatest good for the greatest number.

There are at least two difficulties with this simple-sounding rule. The first is the problem of knowing what the results of an action will be. Utilitarianism is a consequentialist theory—an act is good or bad depending on what flows from it—and to judge the consequences of any act we have to know in advance what those will be. And this requires a predictive model, with all the correspondence problems that go along with one. This has been a criticism of utilitarianism from the beginning.

But even if we could tell the consequences of our acts we still wouldn't know what "good" means. Quantifying pain and pleasure is a hopeless task in itself, not to say an absurd one, but as soon as you step away from a simple calculus of pain you multiply your difficulties and return to the very problem that Bentham tried to eliminate. John Stuart Mill distinguished higher and lower pleasures, claiming that he'd rather be Socrates dissatisfied than a happy fool. But how does Mill know this? And what, after all, is a "higher" pleasure? What is the ranking of a perfectly grilled hamburger compared to a mediocre chateaubriand? A popular novel weighed against a philosophical treatise? Are fireworks, beloved by philosophers as different as Adorno and Murdoch, better or worse than *Madama Butterfly*? How do we relate physical and psychological pain? And why do we rely on well-educated middle-class white males like Mill to draw up the list?

Mill's move is understandable, though, because it's hard to come up with a utilitarian answer to the question of how we should live unless we take it to mean that we should devote ourselves entirely to the amelioration of others' pain. Given the amount of unnecessary suffering in the world, this leads to a life of ascetic self-sacrifice. Bentham's model of humans as pleasure-seeking machines thus ends up requiring us to follow Mother Theresa or Albert Schweitzer. (The contemporary utilitarian Peter Singer draws this conclusion, but neither Bentham nor Mill did, though both were devoted to causes of public welfare.)

These are noble examples, perhaps, but they don't really offer much guidance in the middle ground in which most of us live. Is such a life flawed or unethical? With Mill, at least, we have some advice that makes sense in everyday life: we should read good books, give to respectable charities and help others, listen to uplifting music, and in general act like a good communicant of the Church of England except that we don't have to go to church. The only problem is that we have no justification for any of these guidelines except "the general suffrage of those familiar" with them—that is, consensus.

In fact, utilitarians have difficulty explaining why we should be moral in the first place. They need to tell us why we should strive to reduce the suffering of others instead of (or as well as) our own, because without this additional element Bentham's basic principles are more likely to lead to Hobbes's war of each against all instead of a better world with less suffering. But here, especially, utilitarianism falls short. Michael Slote, explaining and defending it for The Oxford Companion to Philosophy, addresses the topic in parentheses, as if he's trying to slip something by us: "Combining these elements (and adding the assumption that morality requires us to do our best), most current direct (or act-) utilitarians want to say that an act is morally obligatory. . ." And so on. This is disappointing. We expect a theory of ethics to explain why we should do good instead of burying the issue under an assumption. It is hard not to agree with Charles Taylor's conclusion that utilitarianism "speaks from a moral position which it can't acknowledge."[2]

Utilitarianism is not the only important school of ethical thought, of course. There has recently been a strong revival of so-called virtue ethics. The cultivation of certain forms of conduct and habits of response seems to answer one of the objections to a lot of Western ethical thinking, its obsession with clear-cut moments of decision. Virtue ethicists suggest that what is right or wrong about a life is its overall tone, the way our face turns to a loved one in hard times or how we act toward the stranger who's just run over our dog, and that little habits and moments of inattention are in fact highly significant ethically.

But what virtues should we inculcate, and what is the content of each one? Let us assume that the ideal person should exhibit the virtue of courage. Is courage exemplified best by a war protester, a firefighter, a hospice counselor, or a bomber pilot launching cruise missiles whose work day is statistically safer than a commute to the office on the Los Angeles freeways? The very idea of a virtue is a difficult one, and defining any of them is asking for trouble.

Virtue ethics has been kidnapped by conservatives, because it can be adapted very easily to a program of indoctrination. This weakness is endemic; like Mill's higher pleasures, it's hard to define virtues by anything more solid than general agreement. Aristotle built much of this theory on that very basis. (This is only one aspect of his thinking on the subject, but it is the one with the greatest influence on virtue ethics.) His preference was to collect, collate, and examine as many varying opinions on a given issue as possible, which he did with the help of his students at the Lyceum. He would then attempt to determine the rational principle that best fit these theories, thereby "saving the appearances."

In his own field of marine biology this practice could lead to astute functional analyses, but in the human sphere it effectively canonized the actual. The principles that Aristotle derived from his contemporaries' views of course ended up a mere rationalization for a social order identical to the Greek polis. In Alasdair McIntyre's stinging description, the great-souled man of Book IV of the *Nicomachean Ethics*—haughty, condescending, low-voiced, a collector of beautiful useless things who remembers what he has done for others but not what they have done for him—is "very nearly an English gentleman."[3] Aristotle provided an eternal principle to justify common beliefs, an unimpeachably universal justification for a social order little different than the one from which he had started out.

The other dominant school in contemporary ethical philosophy is that of deontological ethics. "Deontological" refers to binding rules, and theorists like Kant and the late John Rawls were looking for rules that could apply universally. Indeed, one of Kant's tests for a genuinely moral act is that it should be something that would be right for everyone to do. There is no hint of relativism here. The first things that have to be thrown aside are the differences between one culture and another.

In fact, Kant argues that even specifically human qualities are themselves to be ignored; the moral law binds all rational beings of whatever kind. Deontologists admit that people (and rational aliens from *Star Trek*) are different in a lot of ways, but they abstract from these differences when building their theories. In Rawls's influential *Theory of Justice* they are concealed behind a "veil of ignorance." By beginning with a subject denuded of all specificity deontologists claim they depend neither on definitions of human nature nor on a belief in an ordered cosmos.

But these theories are just as tied to a specific picture of humanity as any other form of the ethics of what. They model human life as an affair of disembodied, radically separated minds. Kant recognized no moral value in our feelings and none, of course, in conformity to external rules. He held (to quote Rawls) "that a person is acting autonomously when the principles of his action are chosen by him as the most adequate possible expression of his nature as a free and equal rational being."[4] This, of course, is a definition: we are in essence independent rational beings. This inevitably implies an atomized world in which each person determines his or her principles of conduct and then enters a world of others from outside, a world united only by a common commitment to reason. In an age of liberal democracy, capitalist production, and acquisitive individualism this doesn't seem like an inaccurate characterization. But it excludes the very processes in which we create and change each other, and it leaves us with an ethical code fit only for a planet of strangers

> in which the self, shorn of all contingently-given attributes, assumes a kind of supra-empirical status, essentially unencumbered, bounded in advance and given prior to its ends, a

pure subject of agency and possession, ultimately thin. Not
only my character but even my values and deepest convictions
are relegated to the contingent, as features of my condition
rather than constituents of my person.[5]

And this is quite aside from the inadequacy of pure reason as a tool to
chart the world or plot a meaningful course through it. As most critics have noticed, Kant's prescriptions are predominantly negative,
functioning mostly to insure that the rights of others are not limited.
He gives us no idea at all of what a good life would consist of.

The combination of rationalism and atomization gives deontological ethics a bloodless feel. In the *Grounding for the Metaphysic of
Morals* Kant explains that one who acts out of love of his fellows,
deriving satisfaction and happiness from the good he does, is not
acting morally, while a cold-hearted philanthropist with no sympathetic care for others would have "a worth far higher than any that a
good-natured temperament might have" because "he is beneficent,
not from inclination, but from duty."[6] Yet without the ability to listen, respond to, and be changed by the needs of others, how could
such a monster be anything but a Dickensian caricature or a highly
efficient social service organization? What is missing here, most of
all, is the vital texture of people living with each other, and indeed
the objects of Kant's benevolence seem to have no existence at all.

There is a chill at the heart of Kant's vision. He told his students that
"Ethics is no analysis of inclination but a prescription which is contrary
to all inclination."[7] For all the grandeur of moral law, even Kant could
find no persuasive reason to be good rather than bad, and he was forced
to postulate a deity and an afterlife of rewards and punishments:

> Moral laws can be right without a third being [god], but in the
> absence of such a being to make their performance necessary they
> would be empty. Men were right, therefore, in recognizing that the
> absence of a supreme judge would make all moral laws ineffectu-
> al. There would be no incentive, no reward and no punishment.[8]

No benevolent creator would let us discover the moral law and yet leave us without a reason to follow it.

The sad fact is that these three schools have trouble answering the questions we really want to ask: How should we live? Why should we be good? Utilitarianism can't give much of a persuasive answer to any ethical questions. Ever since Aristotle virtue ethics has ended up recommending exactly the qualities favored in whatever culture it came from. And deontological ethics reduces us to an isolated decision-making faculty that looks suspiciously like the defining attribute of the laborer, voter, or consumer in the world of modern capitalism, ignoring the world of human warmth and caring and the subpersonal common life on which we and our decision making truly depend, offering us no positive guidance.

This happens because these starting points imply particular and partial models of experience that we take for the whole. If we start with the life of the Greek city-states, we're going to end up with a streamlined citizen of the Greek city-states. If, more subtly, we start by stripping away all social qualities and peculiarities and begin our theory with an isolated mind deciding on rules of conduct, we end up with a society in which everyone is isolated from everyone else. The ethics of what locks us into circular reasoning. The answers are given even before we ask the questions, because they are the answers assumed by the models themselves.

This approach is so dominant in the West that there may seem to be no other basis for ethics. Charles Taylor, in Sources of the Self, takes it as a given that the "roots of respect for life and integrity" must derive from a theory of what human beings are:

> [T]his "instinct" receives a variable shape in culture, as we have seen. And this shape is inseparable from an account of what it is that commands our respect. The account seems to articulate the intuition. It tells us, for instance, that human beings are creatures of God and made in his image, or that they are immortal souls, or that they are all emanations of

divine fire, or that they are all rational agents and thus have a
dignity that transcends any other being, or some other such
characterization; and that *therefore* we owe them respect.9

But there is another approach. This is the ethics of how. It is implicit
in the work of Carol Gilligan, Nel Noddings, and other so-called fem-
inist ethicists, but was best developed in China at almost exactly the
same time that Plato, Aristotle, and their successors were forging the
Western philosophical tradition, in the explosion of social and philosophical thought of the Warring States period. It does not look for a
definition and shies away from identifying a picture of experience
with experience itself. Instead, it begins with ways in which we create
and change each other, the fundamental patterns of bodily cognition
in which we are embraided with all other creatures.

The ethics of how does not dispense with metaphors. There is no
way it could, because we cannot think without some kind of reduc-
tionism. But not all thinking depends on a picture of an underlying
order of things. Instead of modeling a state and deriving rules or
principles from that model to guide action, the ethics of how regis-
ters processes and aims at harmonizing activity with those processes. Even though there is nothing that we can either contemplate or
refer to in orienting ourselves, the processes we discern shape us
toward a moral way to live. For this reason the Chinese sage does not
see the truth; she *embodies* it. Because there is no separation in classical Chinese thinking between thought and emotion—both of them
come from the *xin*, or "heart/mind"—Chinese morality is more a
matter of affective attunement than a commitment to a code.

The centrality of process, of change and mutual interaction, is a
Chinese commonplace. For millennia its philosophical thought
started from the *I Ching*, or Book of Changes, and in the traditional
interpretation of an obscure part of the *Analects* Confucius says, with
a sigh, "If I could add 50 years to my life, I would study the [Book
of] Changes and become free of error."10 We read in the Great Com-
mentary to the Changes:

Change is indeed broad, and it is great! When we speak of it as
something far-reaching, then there is no stopping it. When
one speaks of it as something near, then it operates calmly and
correctly. When one speaks of it as how it pervades Heaven and
Earth, then it does so with perfect thoroughness. . . . In capa-
ciousness and greatness change corresponds to Heaven and
Earth; in the way change achieves complete fulfillment, change
corresponds to the four seasons . . . and in the efficacy of its
ease and simplicity, change corresponds to perfect virtue. [11]

The Chinese did not talk about a "universe." (Note the singularity
built into the Greek word.) Their usual terms for everything, collec-
tively, were *tian xia*, all under heaven, and *wan wu*, ten thousand
things. Interestingly, *wu* does not mean "objects" so much as it
means those things that interact and transform, a category that
includes people, animals, plants, rivers, and clouds.

This does not mean, of course, that the Chinese thought they
lived in a chaotic mess. They assumed that the mutual transformations of the ten thousand things made up a complicated, ever-chang-
ing harmony. Their world view implied an endless conversation in
which things exist only in their interaction with all others. Everything comes into being and is ceaselessly transformed through these
interactions. The flow of that transformation is *Tao*, the Way, which
is the central metaphor of Chinese thought: the unfathomable and
harmonious current of interactions. The *Tao* is manifest in whatever
happens, but it does not exist aside from this totality. It has its long-
term rhythms such as the seasons and its local propensities, but it is
not an ordering principle that can be abstracted from events. It cannot even be described or named.

The kind of model-building typical of Western theories would be
the wrong way of dealing with this approach. The Chinese were
unwilling to toss the unrepeatable overboard so they could arrive at a
manageable description of things, and they knew that no intellectual
structure could capture the specific constellation of influences

making up each moment. Their ethical orientation could therefore not depend on any kind of rule.

Ethical conduct, instead, is action that participates in the workings of Tao. Within truly good people there is no conflict between desire and nature; their spontaneous acts are in accord with the all-pervading harmony. This is a non-egoistic ideal, but the sage's selfless action is not a religious gift or even an ethical duty, let alone a sacrifice of what is centrally important to us as human beings. The Chinese of this period (and later) assumed that since there was no permanence to anything, ourselves included, there was no real "self" to lose. We realize our lives fully when we act in accord with the way things are, because we ourselves are part of the ten thousand things.

If the fact/value distinction remains here, it is significantly blurred. What is ethical is identical to what is true. The reasoning does not really pass from "is" to "ought," as Hume complains of in Western arguments; the two are equally present at every step. The Chinese approach implies that genuine comprehension of the world and truly ethical conduct are identical. Both can be achieved only through egoless attentiveness, and to accomplish one is to accomplish the other. The only "ought" is that we should experience the world as it is.

How this works out in practice appears best in the *Mencius*, a text that conveniently comes closer than most other classical Chinese works to Western standards of explicitness. Mencius (Mengzi, in Chinese) was Confucius's greatest successor. He is said to have lived from 372 BCE to 289 BCE, when the bloodshed of the Warring States period was reaching its violent climax. Yet he is famous for his insistence that human nature is good. There is something heroic in this belief, which appears to fly in the face of everything that surrounded him. But Mencius did not look to heroes. He pointed, instead, to the fellow-feeling that exists in everyone:

> [N]o man is devoid of a heart sensitive to the suffering of others. . .suppose a man were, all of a sudden, to see a young child on the verge of falling into a well. He would certainly be

> moved to compassion, not because he wanted to get in the
> good graces of the parents, nor because he wished to win the
> praise of his fellow villagers or friends, nor yet because he
> disliked the cry of the child.[12]

This is a matter of a spontaneous emotional response; Mencius does-
n't say that we would drop everything and rush to the baby's rescue.
And he also denies that our reaction points to either calculation or
fear of embarrassment. He is making an assertion about the way
human beings are built: that an immediate impulse of sympathy for
another's distress is one aspect of the way we constitute ourselves.

This is one of four sprouts, as Mencius calls them, which charac-
terize the genuinely human:

> [W]hoever is devoid of the heart of compassion is not
> human, . . .whoever is devoid of the heart of shame is not
> human, whoever is devoid of the heart of courtesy and mod-
> esty is not human, and whoever is devoid of the heart of right
> and wrong is not human. The heart of compassion is the
> germ [sprout] of benevolence; the heart of shame, of dutiful-
> ness; the heart of courtesy and modesty, of observance in the
> rites; the heart of right and wrong, of wisdom. Man has these
> four germs just as he has four limbs.[13]

These are primarily interactional, relational qualities—not the
virtues or ethical maxims of an isolated self. As forms of the activity
of the *Tao* in which we are embraided and thus aspects of our fundamental nature, they lead us to realize the profound processes
through which we constitute each other, in both senses of the word:
to understand and to make real.

Spontaneous sympathy is an easy emotion to accept. Others of
the four sprouts may be more difficult for us. Mencius locates the
sense of righteousness in the experience of shame, and these days
we denigrate shame in favor of guilt. Guilt, we are told, promotes

autonomy and responsibility, while shame enforces a culture of conformism. But this hardly seems a fair characterization of the Confucian vision. Neither Confucius nor Mencius had any use for the con-
ventionally pious townsmen "who follow the current customs and
consent to the vices of the age."[14] Such "acceptable men" are
"thieves of virtue."[15] The anonymous students who assembled the
Analects included in that work's first paragraph the clearly polemical
question, "if people do not recognize me and it doesn't bother me,
am I not a Superior Man?" Quietism, indifference, and fatalism are
misleading stereotypes of Chinese attitudes.

But what else did Mencius mean by shame, and what did he expect
it to do? We are so averse to shame that we are more likely to experience defensiveness instead: our heart tightens and our chest puffs a little, and we immediately try to justify our conduct. We do not like to
admit that we have fallen short of others' expectations, and we hesitate
to recognize the pain they have experienced at our hands. But these
admissions can be invaluable teachers, most exacting in our intimate
relations with friends, lovers, and family members. To the extent that
we deafen ourselves to shame by self-righteous defensiveness, we lose
the opportunity for responding in a truly human fashion to those we
have harmed, for the painful education of the heart/mind, and for full
awareness of and participation in the currents of our own lives.

It is the same with humility and deference, which emerge in the
respect we pay to family. These, too, can seem alien virtues. But everyone knows that sense of deference, if only in memories of childhood,
just as anyone with a child or younger sibling can recover the emotions of solicitude, care, and delight that they inspired. Mencius says:

> An infant carried in the arms has no lack of knowledge of
> how to love its parents, and when it gets older, it knows auto-
> matically how to respect its older siblings.[16]

The deference this shows us is a lived comprehension of how we
make each other within the examples, patterns, rituals, habits, and

language of our ancestors. These are inescapable; and until we accept our rootedness we cannot take a single step that is truly our own.

The final sprout seems the most confusing; if we already know right and wrong, why do we need the other three sprouts? Franklin Perkins, in an unpublished paper, has pointed out that "the sense of right and wrong" refers literally to the ability to discriminate. We should read this passage as "the heart/mind that can distinguish clearly is the beginning of wisdom." Mencius explicitly compares this quality with an archer's skill[17], and it is etymologically connected with the term for one of the abilities on which he prided himself:

> Ch'ou asked, "What do you mean when you say 'I understand language'?" Mencius said, "When I hear deceptive speech, I know what it is covering up. When I hear licentious speech, I know its pitfalls. When I hear crooked speech, I know where it departs from the truth. When I hear evasive speech, I know its emptiness...."[18]

At least one part of the "wisdom" we acquire by attending to the way we discriminate is insight into the complexity of ourselves and others and into deception and self-deception. This would explain why Mencius remarked that the wisdom in which Confucius surpassed others equally wise was the perfect appropriateness of all his actions.[19]

Throughout the Confucian tradition we are asked to "extend" our responses from family to friends, from friends to community, and so on. That this is not a process of reasoning by analogy may be seen in the following story. The King of Ch'i wonders if he has the capacity for virtuous leadership, and Mencius tries to reassure him:

> "[Y]ou were sitting up in the main hall and a man walked past the lower part leading an ox. You saw this and asked: 'What are you doing with the ox?' He replied: 'We are going to consecrate a bell with its blood.' You said: 'Let it go—I can't stand to see the agony on its face, like that of an inno-

cent person going to execution!' The man then answered:
'Shall we forget the consecration of the bell?' You said: 'How
can it be forgotten? Substitute it with a sheep!' ...

"What you did was an act of humanity. You saw the ox, but
had not seen the sheep. When it comes to animals, if the
Superior Man has seen them while alive, he cannot stand to
watch them die. If he hears their screams, he cannot stand to
eat their meat. Therefore he stays away from the kitchen."[20]

This story seems strange to us, but we must realize that Mencius is
not advocating a kind of willed ignorance. He and the king saw ritual sacrifice and meat eating as human necessities; it would have been
impossible to dispense with either. What is important about this
conversation is Mencius's evident belief that compassion arises on
its own when one is in the presence of suffering, almost as if it were
a contagion. To extend compassion it is necessary only to open oneself more and more to the unhappiness of others.

It is all too obvious that few people live this way, and like anyone
who asserts the goodness of humanity Mencius is forced to explain
evil. In the famous parable of Ox Mountain[21] he attributes ethical
insensitivity to the social environment, and much of his explicit
political advice is directed toward ensuring that all people will have
ample food and shelter; only then will it be possible for a sage-king
to lead them to virtue. He also suggests that unethical conduct is a
kind of error, telling the king of Ch'i that the pursuit of authority by
military power instead of by virtue and sane social policy is "like
climbing a tree to catch a fish."[22]

This seems close to Socrates' dictum that nobody knowingly
does wrong. But we should remember the difference between the
two thinkers' worlds. For Socrates the truth had a sort of supraper-
sonal existence discernible by reasoned inquiry—though it is hard
for us now to clarify the details of his position, if indeed it was ever
explicitly or consistently stated. Because of this externality and

because people (or at least all healthy free males) were capable of reason, they could all be brought to a vision of the good.

Mencius's notion of the truth is not similarly intellectualistic. There is no site in which one can encounter the *Tao* apart from the everyday world of actions and responses. If one "loses one's original mind," taking the fraudulent world of wealth, pleasure, and power for the real one, one also loses sensitivity to the actions of *Tao*, which are the shaping and motivating forces that bring one back to that genuine nature. Recovery is an arduous process of self-transformation, unaided by any guiding vision of an eternal truth. It is something like trying to do a jigsaw puzzle without the picture on the box.

Is Mencius thus closer to Aristotle, who was also concerned with the lasting effects of upbringing and environment? Here, too, the differences are more telling than the apparent similarities. Aristotle's practical wisdom—*phronesis*—is "natural" only within his teleological understanding of the human species. It arises not within the original mind but from the self as project—we must shape ourselves through reason and example, because we rise to humanity only after long discipline and repeated practice. As we have seen, this means that Aristotle must look to a model of some sort for definitions and exemplars of virtue, and his account therefore depends on the unspoken assumptions of his own culture.

Mencius's own thought is not immune to this problem. He and Confucius both believed that the rituals supposedly handed down from the sage-kings of antiquity gave one access to the workings of *Tao* and were to be maintained forever. The legendary conservatism of the Confucian tradition is bound up with this belief. But because the rites are only one vehicle for a process also accessible through the four sprouts and their concomitant virtues, they do not define ethical conduct the way Aristotle's *phronesis* does. The replication of social forms, though important, is logically less central to Confucian ethics. This also means that any model of existence that may be implicit in the rites should not be taken for a picture of reality. In a startling piece of philosophical anthropology Mencius explains funeral ritual by the horror felt when "the most ancient" children encountered foxes and wildcats devouring the bodies of their dead parents.[23] The necessary conclusion is that the spontaneous response leads to the ritual, not the other way around.

Although he was criticized even in his own day for his belief in the fundamental goodness of humanity, Mencius remained confident that only the path of virtue could lead to the inexhaustible accumulation of ch'i, the breath that is one physical manifestation of the workings of Tao. Acting in accordance with Tao is effortless and profoundly delightful. This is perhaps the best reason he gives for being virtuous: that delicately vulnerable expansion of spirit we feel at another's smile of satisfaction is a true token of the Way, and though not definitive of virtue (as the moral sentiment school thought) the iridescence of our emotional life is at least confirming evidence that some acts are indeed virtuous:

> If one delights in them then they grow. If they grow then how can they be stopped? If they cannot be stopped then one does not notice one's feet dancing to them, one's hands swaying to them.[24]

Mencius also shared the view, found in a wide range of Warring States sources, that clear perception, efficacious action, and moral conduct are identical. The perturbations introduced by acts posed against nature are eventually lost in the vast movements of Tao. One is therefore more successful when one acts in agreement with its activities, and acting against it requires a lot of energy; this is why military empires never last. (In the short run one can get away with this, and Mencius would have had to admit that all too many vicious characters manage a peaceful death before their stratagems collapse.)

This threefold identity does not mean that the ten thousand things are organized by any ethical principle, though the neo-Confucianism of Zhu Xi, more than a millennium later, tends in this direction. It means, instead, that Heaven's heedlessness of our egoistic demands and our existence within the mutual interactions of all under Heaven require us to act out of a deep recognition of our mutual dependence and vulnerability. At the same time, this aligns us with the movements of Tao so, like the sage in the Book of Changes, we can "perfectly emulate the transformations of Heaven and Earth." François Jullien, in an excellent book on Mencius and Western ethical thought, puts it this way:

> Beginning with this visible sprout, flowering unexpectedly but undeniably in my experience through reactions of shame or pity, I can climb steadily, by following that thread through all experience, to the unconditioned foundation [of all things]. Because, in the opposite sense, my nature can be nothing other than an individuation of the great processes of the world and my moral responses are its immediate manifestation; that is why the spontaneity of that emotion places me in direct communication with that which never ceases, in its principle, to move and animate all things.[25]

The most profoundly human way we can live is the way in which we are most sensitive to the transformations of Tao, and vice versa.

What specific path leads to Mencius's "floodlike" ch'i? The apparent emptiness of his four virtues—their lack of defined content—is not a defect. He acknowledges no model that yields reliable prognostications, no order underlying the operations of Tao that we can consult; as in the (nonphilosophical) classical world, there is no "outside" from which we can see the whole. There is, therefore, no privileged viewpoint—not even privileged access to our own thoughts—which could support any ideology of domination. All that can be known from our part in the ten thousand things is how completely we are responsible for each other. Mutual dependence and sympathy, our vulnerability and responsibility for the pain we cause, the importance of the past out of which we constitute ourselves, and our own ability to discriminate, reflect, and analyze others and our selves are all drawn from that realization. Mencius's virtues are a stance rather than a set of rules; and they grow not through the contemplation or application of principles but from extending the basic ways of being that grew in us, if we were fortunate, within our family life.

We destroy or deform that process of growth if we try to define the good. Instead of speeding our progress to the virtuous state, overt ethical ideals act like a Procrustean bed to which we force our natural goodness to conform, and this is another reason Mencian ethics is never prescriptive:

> [You have] not yet understood Righteousness, [if you regard] it as something external. You must be willing to work at it, understanding that you cannot have precise control over it. You can't forget about it, but you can't force it to grow, either.

> You don't want to be like the man from Sung. There was a man from Sung who was worried about the slow growth of his crops and so he went and yanked on them to accelerate their growth. Empty-headed, he returned home and announced to his people: "I am so tired today. I have been out stretching the crops." His son ran out to look, but the crops had already withered.[26]

This may serve as a Mencian judgment on the ethics of what.

The ethics of how is preeminently concerned with the texture of a life, with the small turnings that may lead us unawares to a place we would never want to be. It may not help us think through the problems in an ethics exam; but then sitting down in front of a fact pattern from someone else's life fails to reproduce the complex texture of entwined feelings that animate the major decisions we are really called on to make. This is not to say that such choices fell outside the Chinese understanding of ethics. Although Herbert Fingarette, in an influential book, argued that Confucius had no concept of moral choice, Mencius certainly did:

Mencius said, "I like fish and I like bear's paw, but if I have to choose between them, I will let go of the fish and take the bear's paw. I like life and I like Righteousness. But if I have to choose between them I will let go of life and take Righteousness. I want life, but there are things more important to me than life. Therefore there are things that I won't do just to live. I hate death, but there are things that I hate more than death, and thus there are certain kinds of suffering that I won't avoid...."[27]

I do not want to minimize the weaknesses of this position. Mencius's great antagonist within the Confucian tradition, Xunzi, argued that humans were evil and needed to be shaped by ritual to a semblance of virtue, and Xunzi's harshness reminds us of how consistently Chinese history turned to despotism. It is too easy to mistake a pseudo-benevolent tyranny for virtuous leadership, at least in the medium term, and it may well be implicit in Mencius's approach that there can be no claim for the weak once one loses sight of our mutual vulnerability.

For the sake of balance, I should also note that notions of individual rights and broadly based representative democracy don't appear in the Western tradition until the eighteenth century. And formulating rules of conduct, such as we have tried to do in the ethics of what, has created its own problems: how to justify those rules, how to apply them in everyday life, and how to avoid tying them to fixed interpretations of the past. The ethics of how avoids these problems. It offers an orientation to our lives that does not depend on the logical elaboration of universal truths. In addition, it suggests that the disappearance of a "hypergood" object of attraction or even worship would not be fatal to a genuinely illuminating ethical philosophy, as Taylor seems to hold. As we come to see the limited role of discursive thought in our activity and how deeply rooted we are in the subpersonal and selfless processes of bodily cognition Mencius should prove a welcome companion.

Consequences

7. THE LAST MAN STANDING

THAT ENDLESSLY ANATOMIZED and problematic object—the modern self—so central and so beleaguered, has at least three separate roots: the ancient stress on the self as a project, the assertion of a point outside the world from which experience could be grasped as a whole, and the construction through language of an orienting model elaborated from that starting point. But these are only part of the story. We cannot think of the self today without its other, the omnipresent and imperious realm of the social. The social, too, has a history, by no means tied in an uncomplicated fashion to that of the self, and the only way to appreciate the character of self-experience in the contemporary Western world is to see how these different histories interact.

The self as project is by far the oldest of these. To choose a way of life and then pose it against the changes of time—to make one's fate—has been an ideal in the West for close to three thousand years. It is already present among Homer's heroes, who justified their privileges by a willingness to risk their lives for honor and the defense of "their" people. Often this project culminated in a "beautiful death," the refusal to be deterred from duty or the obligations of glory by the certainty that one will die. The prototype for this is Achilles, who chooses his fate and embraces the death that will give him immortality in the poets' songs—the only real immortality found in the *Iliad*, though other stories granted him and a few other heroes eternal life in the Islands of the Blessed.

The ideal of the Homeric warrior was eventually absorbed into the civic culture of the *polis*. The conduit for this was likely military. The Greek city may have thrived by trade, but it saw itself as a military unit, and service in the army was an essential part of citizenship—witness Alcibiades's praise of Socrates the soldier in the *Symposium*. The beautiful death was no longer the test of the aristocratic warrior's love of glory, commemorated in the *kleos* of epic poetry and a tomb to recall his deeds. It becomes civic virtue: the sacrifice of the citizen-soldier for the city. And the self as project can be traced from here through ever less warlike forms, into the therapeutic and soteriological schools of classical philosophy, the mystery cults and the emphasis on contributions to civic life, and the late antique "care of the self" that interested Foucault in his last years. In all these various shapes it plays a major role in the ideology and spiritual practice of the Hellenistic kingdoms and the Roman Empire.

The civic virtue of the Empire did not require military service; the legions were professionals, no longer the citizen-soldiers of the republic. Instead, it entailed devotion to one's city and its gods through government service, sometimes lucrative but often punishingly expensive; the erection of public amenities such as theaters and baths; the provision of banquets and games for one's fellows; and simply bearing children to perpetuate "the common city of gods and men." In the ethical revival so heavily and successfully promoted by Augustus a code of public probity and family morality was added to these obligations. Their most direct descendants are the civic humanism of the Renaissance and the Jeffersonian ideals that were central to the ideology of the new United States. But the self as project was carried into later history primarily in the religious form it acquired in late antiquity. Within a Christianized culture of self-examination and aspiration to holiness the explicit ideal became a self of divinely inspired inner unity, coherence, direction, and dedication.

Whatever shape it takes, the self in the history of the West has always been posed against nature and the corrosion of time. The archaic hero showed his contempt for death by accepting its inevitability. The disciplined life of the polis was routinely contrasted with the state of nature, which the Greeks thought unfit for human beings. And for the Christian, of course, the natural world is a fallen one, to be endured as a test until the soul returns to its divine home. How much Greek thought contributed to the doctrine of original sin is a question that goes well beyond the scope of this essay; but it is striking that for both Greeks and Christians the proper choice of life set people in tension with their biological existence.

This much is likely old news, though it is worth stressing that the nature/culture opposition is itself a cultural artifact. The correlative cosmology of the Chinese, for example, may look like Mediaeval and Renaissance systems of analogy between microcosm and macrocosm, but the Chinese were tracing resonances and echoes among equally natural phenomena while the Europeans sought signs of a divine order hidden in the created world. The Chinese system obscures the differences between its terms and aims at an alignment with the nature of things. The Western model insists on their separation and strives to transcend, interpret, command, or transform the merely natural, privileging the one true order of the divine.

In its Christian form the self as project thus merges with the notion of an external or transcendent perspective from which one can grasp the real and rational order of things. This, too, is no more a universal aspiration than is the self tensed against the biological, nor do people inevitably look for such a perspective when religious traditions are naturalized. Bronze Age Chinese, like the Greeks, had interrogated the gods through divination. The philosophical schools of the Warring States period, though, redefined truth as the tendency of the unknowable Tao. In a manner misleadingly reminiscent of Hegel, the absolute vanished as a separate category of existence and was incarnated as the immanent order of all under heaven. Invisibly present in the everyday but utterly inexpressible, Heaven did not speak and could no longer be addressed. The harmony and order of all under heaven was neither an eternal or unchanging pattern nor anything that could be described or expressed in a rational system.

The naturalization of religion in Greek philosophy was much more straightforward. The truth once sought through divination and the inspired visions of poetry was now pursued through reason, which inherited the religious function of revealing an absolute order separate from but somehow inherent in the world of experience—hence its divine nature. In the common culture of the pagan Empire reason had been an instrumentally useful ability which, though valuable, could give no access to truth. With Plato, and even more with the assimilation of Platonic philosophy to Christianity, reason became a foundational as well as a structuring element of a model, founded on innately known or revealed truth, which could be used to grasp the world in thought. Christianity rejected the directionless rationality of the Stoics; like a caricature of Plato at his most dogmatic the church asserted that the truth could indeed be known and in fact was now in the church's possession. Yet the gulf between rational order and experience (and between theory and practice, among others) remained. It has been accepted by the Greeks and by us their successors as self-evident; but it is instead an artifact of a specific process, a secularization of the structure of the religious world of archaic Greece.

It was Christianity that cemented the unity of the self as project and the need for certainty with the last of the three background elements of the history of the Western self, the centrality of discourse. The church now provided both the intellectual equipment and the justification for the self as a grounded, articulated, and considered project. Our estrangement from god generated the impetus for defined needs and goals, and revelation provided the rock outside the buzzing confusion of everyday life on which an orienting model of reality could be built. But the model could be built only in language, in rational discourse.

In the Christian West, where matters of doctrine play a central part in everyday religion compared with life in the Orthodox East, these concerns and forms of experience have been of more than technical, philosophical interest. They are implicit and often explicit in preaching, popular devotional texts, and in the structure of religious experience even among the laity. Self-knowledge becomes a religious duty going beyond mere introspection. In order to obtain absolution one must be able to give the confessor a verbal account of one's own conduct and one's own thoughts. (In contrast, the traditional Jewish confession in the Yom Kippur service is a laundry list of faults, recited in heterophonic unison by the entire congregation.) The discursive self, projected against the vicissitudes of life on foundations of certainty, constructed through constant reflective scrutiny, stretched toward a future state in which all will be known and everything coherent, is no longer the exclusive possession of a spiritual elite. It is the pattern we all draw upon. Thanks to Christianity we are all philosophers.

The modern self is made from these three elements at least. But conventional histories of the self leave out its social context. We do not experience our lives as detached activity in a void. Most of the time we feel ourselves confronting an autonomous corporate body, the social world, which makes demands in its own name and with which we must come to terms to secure some psychic territory for our authentic lives. We pose our selves against this as much as against the depredations of time and natural dangers.

Without a parallel account of Western ideas of the social world any history of the self is dangerously incomplete. The problem, however, is that there is very little of this history to be told. Scholars did not seem to spend much time thinking about "the social" until the recent past; the first use of the word "society" as the personified activity of a community comes in the late eighteenth century, and the term "sociology" dates from 1830. (It was an invention of Auguste Comte's.)

These concepts emerge only as providential theories of history and community recede. Christianity is thus as important in the history of the social as it is in the history of the self, but it plays a strikingly different and more complex role. Instead of creating a new synthesis with Classical elements—which is what happened with ideas about the self—Christian social thought all but abolished the Greek and Roman readings of common experience and fashioned a very different one in their place, the paradoxical and almost self-contradictory notion of providential order.

In the polis the community as a whole was posed against nature, and the self as project took its shape within that context; even Jaeger noted the "public" quality of the Greek conscience. This rendition of experience was little affected by changes in the political power of urban elites and the social and economic relations of the Roman Empire, and its survival made possible the Empire's reliance on local aristocracies for administration. Far into the "decline of Rome" most literate Greeks and Romans remained committed to their cities and the Empire as common projects.

There was, as well, no accepted perspective outside the community from which a different way of life could be elaborated. Self and city were created together within traditional models that were understood to be provisional; but since certainty lay outside human powers, those models were also immune from radical critique. Humanity could pose nothing against one partial truth except another truth that was equally partial.

The church may appear to carry on this structure, and it often saw itself as a corporate body in the image of Noah's ark: the company of the saved voyaging through tests posed by a loving but strict deity. But the ark does not contain a community, only those individuals deemed worthy of salvation. There is a fundamental difference between the classical city and the Christian church. In the former the ties between people are primary and foundational; we are political animals, whose nature it is to live with others. The Christian community, on the other hand, exists only secondarily. One is first of all an individual working out his or her relationship with the creator. Membership in the church arises from that relationship and is subordinate to it.

This is a crucial change. Christianity had set itself against the city, dissolving its ties and reconstructing life on entirely individualist lines, and henceforth the community was justified only insofar as it fostered one's spiritual growth. If it failed in this purpose, it was rejected. To take one's shape from one's social being risked moral failure, so the individual's relationship to social life became distanced, critical, and essentially opportunistic.

In this kind of account no independent explanation of social life is needed. The only realities are god and the individual soul. Lines of authority and aspiration run between the individual and the divine. So, too, do the lines of explanation. Relations among people and among their kingdoms on earth dissolve when seen with the eye of faith to reveal a set of vertical relations whose purpose is god's alone.

And god is concerned above all with the fate of individuals. Under the appearance of mass movements, changes in technology and learning, wars and philosophical debates lies the reality of his shaping involvement in the life of each person, often manifest in the ironic twists of the historical record. (In another version of this approach god's concern was limited to the moral education of the sovereign, whose subjects suffered with him as a kind of collateral damage.) The limited opening that antique culture offered for social thought and the study of specifically social experience thus disappeared with the dissolution of classical civic culture.

It was generally accepted even into the seventeenth century that this was the ultimate explanation for human events. Clarendon's history of the English Civil War is overtly providentialist and so, famously, is Bossuet's universal history. The theory was wearing thin by the time of the "European crisis of conscience" that preceded the Enlightenment, and Bossuet's explanation that the great empires of the ancient world existed solely to administer lessons to god's chosen people was bound to excite derision. But the vitality of providentialism should not be underestimated, and its potential for rhetorical power and moral grandeur survived into the nineteenth century and underpins Lincoln's magnificent second inaugural address.

What was lost with the providentialist explanation is evident in the Enlightenment inability to describe historical movement, something that might otherwise seem inexplicable. History had great prestige in the eighteenth century, and men as important as Voltaire and Hume devoted much time to large-scale historical works. (Hume wrote his history of England for money, but he took his task seriously.) Popularizations and vulgarizations abounded, and hackwork such as Rollin's ancient histories and Volney's late and fashionably "philosophical" *Les Ruines* were staples of provincial presses until well into the 1800s. Yet of all this production only Gibbon is still read. Huge amounts of research went into the best of the century's historical writing, but the books have no interpretation to offer that is worth our attention. In spite of good intentions, in spite of their scholarship, and in spite of attempts to judge others by appropriate standards, eighteenth-century historians seem to have missed something vital.

The problem with their work was not the lack of an historical sense. What it lacked was a social sense. Once the hand of god was removed from the providential model one was left with abstract individuals in a conceptual vacuum. With the partial exception of the Catholic and heterodox Vico, none of the age's thinkers could conceive of a replacement for the discarded system. The idea of a culture constituting itself through its own interactions was completely alien to their thought.

God no longer meddled with the daily affairs of the world. His role was now that of the watchmaker whose genius was shown in the working out through time of causes he set in motion at the creation. The history of human institutions was similarly reconceived. For Montesquieu, to take one example, they were the products of watchmaker legislators who set social mechanisms in motion to run on their own:

> At the birth of societies, the leaders of republics create the
> institutions; thereafter, it is the institutions that form the
> leaders of republics.[1]

History is reduced to a kind of historical anthropology. Growth and decay, decline and fall, conquest and defeat—these are the social changes describable within this model. Reformation, in the strict sense of the word, is also possible. Transformation is not.

It is only after the quarter century of conflict started by the French Revolution that we begin to see the notion of "the social." Several paths led to its emergence. There was the memory of the vast spontaneous movements of the revolutionary years. Conservative organicism was one response, a reactionary corporatism justified by the need for order, not by the command of god—though plentiful amounts of incense, hellfire, and religious rhetoric were deployed to increase its authority. Rational systems of society like Fourier's and Saint-Simon's occupied a kind of middle ground. There was the new theory of collective social constitution advanced by both the right-wing historical schools of Germany and the left-wing German Hegelians, for whom neither culture nor national identity were conscious creations. Seen on the model of language, which as the German legal historian Savigny said existed "only through a series of uninterrupted transformations," they were the product of the unconscious activity of the *Volksgeist*. One final contributor was British political economy, which analyzed economic activity as a sphere with its own life and logic often at odds with the intentions of the individuals involved, a paradox brought out in the moral of Mandeville's *Fable of the Bees*: "private vices, public benefits."

It was Marx who first fused many of these elements. What he also saw with great clarity, especially in his early years, was the historic uniqueness of the emergence of a "social" sphere. But the triumph of capitalism was already transforming the landscape of experience, and the rupture between personal and social soon receded from theoretical scrutiny to become a quasi-biological fact. Marx's insight into its ideological nature came too late to be credible. His liberal critics and many of his epigones were to address the social as it presented itself under capitalism, as if it were a world in itself.

Here, too, we can see intimate connections between philosophical theory and common experience. The dialectic of self and social is enough in the foreground of our lives to become a staple of the popular arts. A wide variety of plots are derived from it: the rebel or pioneer, often destroyed by an uncaring or hostile world, as in *Easy*

Rider, or glamorous in criminality the way Harry Lime far outshines the decent but dull Joseph Cotton character in The Third Man; the "little man" as a cog in the machine (King Vidor's The Crowd remains the archetype of this subgenre); or the individual who sacrifices his own fulfillment for the progress of the whole, a favorite theme of John Ford's—think of Henry Fonda dancing at the half-built church at the end of My Darling Clementine, or John Wayne's Tom Donophan in The Man Who Shot Liberty Valance, late echoes of classical civic virtue but with unclassical doses of pathos.

These films reflect our own dilemma. On the one hand we are granted the most awe-inspiring powers. As autonomous rational beings we must think for ourselves. In the context of our history this means that we must construct a usable model of experience from the standpoint of an authoritative self. We are expected to choose goals and to craft our lives so we can achieve them—in other words, to project a self in which to live out our days against the constraints of the world as we perceive it. Accepting a social role is an abdication of our human calling. The self as project is thus no longer an ideal. It has become an obligation.

But these vast powers of self-creation and autonomy crumble at a touch, like ash, because real activity and agency reside in the incomparably more powerful realm of the social. Man proposes, god disposes, it was said; but these days it is the social world that allows or bars the fulfillment of whatever dreams we hope to realize. This goes far beyond the inevitable conflicts between our desires and those of others. All the wishes and needs of the rest of the world's people come to us summarized and unified into the apparently objective demands of the social. Its word is law, and from its decree no appeal is possible. It is as impassive as fate. Each one of us faces this faceless and heartless tyrant as an isolated being. Paradoxically, the most common experience in the modern Western world is that of being the last person left standing.

The divide between personal and social that tears our lives apart is the result of the same kind of process that cast alienated human activity into heaven, as Marx understood; in both religion and the individual/social split of the modern world each one of us, in isolation, confronts our own collective activity as if it were something apart from and even opposed to ourselves. But there are important differences between religious and social alienation. The individual/social split arises from, reproduces, and justifies the world shaped by capitalist production and alienated labor. The belief in a providential order, originating in a premodern world, is less dependent on the specific character of capitalism, and in fact was its most persuasive within the complex unity of the Middle Ages. It gave at least symbolic access to the social, while the concept of the social, paradoxically, does not.

Christianity maintained the fundamental identity of individual and social experience. The self as project might be posed against nature and against the city, but a single purpose lay behind our inner lives and whatever we encountered in the world of others. Although to our eyes there seemed to be a vast disharmony between the two, their real unity in the subpersonal was explicitly asserted in theology and implicitly assumed in prayer. It might be revealed in a voice from heaven or established as an irrefutable insight. In these and other ways Christianity held together what it had first cut apart.

In the post-Christian world even this quasi-realization of the identity of personal and social is lost. Theories of secular history are more persuasive than Bossuet's, and we can now treat the social as something knowable in itself. But these advantages come at a high price. They cost us Christianity's comprehension, mystified though it was, that social life and the lives of individuals cannot be reduced one to the other but are aspects of a single process.

The post-Christian world is thus incoherent in a way the Christian one was not. Once the mansions of the divine are occupied by human institutions there seems to be nothing external to which one can look for certainty. It's culture all the way up. We have not abandoned the need for certainty, though; the search has just moved in the other direction. The private conscience becomes the cultural space within which the essential is revealed. But since social and individual are now separated at the root, the voice inside the head is not the still, small voice of god; it is either one's inner self to which we must attend or the internalized command of the social that we must resist.

Because we no longer expect that introspection and perception will reveal different aspects of a higher unity, we are caught up in a constant struggle between the purposes we find or create within ourselves and those we discern in the demands of the social. Indeed, if we come across evidence of social processes in introspection we worry that we are losing our authentic character. We can call nothing our own except for the abstract individuality inherited from the Enlightenment project and the autonomous choices we make.

But even these choices are problematic. How can we be certain that they are truly our own and not merely manifestations of socialized and thus inauthentic being? What standards do we have to distinguish the two? Since self-definition is based on separation from the social, we oscillate between our claim to be independent from the world and our fear of being crushed by it, exalted and negated at the same time. The formation of an authentic character thus entails eternal vigilance, constant scrutiny of motives and actions, and a perpetual search for the fundamental, a kernel of indubitable self-nature.

The attempt to sever the seamless workings of subpersonal bodily interaction into personal and social spheres is necessarily self-defeating. Once we separate inner life from our social existence the notion of a complexly textured self with substantial content becomes insupportable, because the realization of that complexity is inevitably social. The motivation for all our preferences become suspect, and the inward spiral of self-examination thus draws the social deeper and deeper into the soul until the ego stands isolated as a null point. However it is construed, the individual is reduced to an abstract being, whether as a bundle of physical urges or a bare faculty of choice. The *me* in its most profoundly authentic form turns out to be the lowest common denominator of human animals. Individualism is the enemy of individuality.

In short, by our self-identification with conscious experience and our reliance on thinkable, graspable orienting models we have cut ourselves off from the processes whereby we constitute each other. Thinking exists today not as a rendition of an all-encompassing providential design but as a withdrawal from the subpersonal activity of the body. It had once tied together heaven and earth by replicating divine discourse, but now it starts from and exhausts the experience that is ascribed to the individual. It therefore pushes ceaselessly against the mutual transformations of the body, which are experienced as either raw urges or the external demands of social life. We are split in two. To the extent that we see ourselves as conscious thinking subjects, our own bodily life confronts us as the alien within.

Instead of living we spend our time inspecting the activities of our lives. We are our own Hanes lady, the one who boasts, "It doesn't say Hanes until I say it says Hanes," and like real-life inspectors on the assembly line we pass judgment on products over which we have little or no control. Whatever we do is offered for our own consideration and approval; the inner I becomes the inner eye, yet another form of the ocular metaphor for understanding that has been a constant of Western thought since Plato. As in every other version of that metaphor, the seer is defined by his or her distance from the object of vision and the object is defined by the presumption that it is unaffected by being observed. In a miserable irony, we have achieved Aristotle's ideal of a life spent largely in contemplation, but instead of eternal truths we end up contemplating our thoughts and our property.

This is not an intellectual error or an accidental by-product of a neutral process. Our transformation is exactly what is called for in today's human order; it both underpins and is maintained by the same structures of production that have remade the world in the image of the market. The problem is not one of too much socialization, or of socialization to the wrong things, or of too great an involvement in the intoxicating spectacle of the modern media, or a manipulation of the contents of the media by governments or by corporate interests. It is that we are mutating into the species best fitted to the capitalist world, and enough remains of our old life that we find the process painful.

Not that there aren't palliatives. Christianity presented human estrangement in a powerfully extreme form but offered, as consolation, the assurance that a better reality lay behind our bodily experience. Now, however, capitalism in the industrialized West has a different solution to an even keener form of the same heartache. It has deployed a more acceptable reality for our benefit, interposed in front of experience instead of behind it. The self as project has become the self as do-it-yourself project, with a wide range of lives now available ready-made. A popular book, not at all shoddy or thoughtless, is titled *Creating a Life Worth Living*. Every afternoon Oprah Winfrey gives self-improvement tips on her television show, and her monthly magazine, called simply *O*, offers further advice to help us live our "best lives." Sporting clubs, Hollywood, the music industry and television provide endless tightly structured dramas of market-tested emotional impact that support, shape, and substitute for experience itself. In recent years warfare has been added to this industry's products, at least in the United States, where the blood and brains of collaterally damaged foreigners are carefully edited out before the evening news.

It is too easy to mock. The lifestyle market, the emotional wallpaper of the popular arts, the obsessive search for an authentic life cannot be taken at face value, but they speak to genuine issues. Capitalist modernity exhibits neither an uncomplicated relationship between needs and fulfillment nor an arbitrary collage of diversionary images. It offers us illusory means to satisfy illusory forms of real needs.

Vissi d'arte: I lived for art, as Tosca sings. Commercial media and the carnival of consumption are only broader, more vulgar and more resource-intensive realizations of the modernist ambition to replace life with ideas. And it is consumption, especially, through which the promise of this new world is ceaselessly dangled before us. High art has become commodified and increasingly shallow, but in compensation, as it were, consumer goods have acquired spiritual depth.

This is something new, though it is not completely without precedent. Only the puritanical or nostalgic refuse to recognize that objects have long been pursued for reasons other than their usefulness. In every stratified society luxury goods are valued as evidence of status or wealth, and new extravagances and more refined styles must be introduced whenever the lower orders gain access to the luxuries of past years. Even in less unequal communities people prefer objects that are attractive, well-made, and pleasurable to use, for reasons obvious to anyone who has owned an inexpensive screwdriver, bicycle, or kitchen knife.

But it would be equally unrealistic to ignore the extent to which all objects today are marketed for the emotional connotations raised by their styling, packaging, and advertising. Cars, toothpaste, flavored creamers for coffee, portable electronics, and toilet paper are sold with promises of ease, of fun, of sexual attraction, and of all the other goods we can imagine. That is why it is not enough for commodities to be simply well-made, utilitarian, efficient, or even beautiful. They are bought for the psychological benefits that their possession promises, and if they lack this quasi-erotic aura they are yanked off the shelves and replaced by sexier ones.

The eroticism of goods is no accident. With common life eliminated from experience the single potency left us is sexual, and the one social act which can be felt directly as social is what we revealingly term sexual intercourse. In a lover's arms we are momentarily released from the stifling and isolating web of words and calculation; but the misery of the rest of life weighs like a nightmare on the delight of sexual congress, vastly enhancing its significance, power, and danger. Sexuality thus spills into and transforms every other form of desire until all of everyday life is eroticized and a state of perpetual tumescence becomes the ideal.

Like the erotic, materialism is an affair not of our flesh but our heads. Our conscious and semiconscious intentions seek their ends through the emotional penumbrae of the products offered for sale. The new world is made up of ideas, images, and symbols of delight and freedom and the fulfillment of all our longings, things far more malleable than the obdurate processes of the body in which we are linked with all others. But those ideas and symbolic actions are never sufficiently rooted in our subpersonal life to give us the satisfactions they promise; in Debord's terms:

> The spectacle is a permanent opium war which aims to make people identify goods with commodities and satisfaction with survival that increases according to its own laws. But if consumable survival is something which must always increase, this is because it continues to contain privation. If there is nothing beyond increasing survival, if there is no point where it might stop growing, this is not because it is beyond privation, but because it is enriched privation.[2]

The spiral of consumption in which each purchase geometrically multiplies the demand for further ones drives the engine of capitalism and strip mines our physical environments and our inner lives at the same time.

This is the very heart of Marx's concept of alienation; he himself notes in the *Economic and Philosophical Manuscripts of 1844* that "estranged labor estranges man from his own body."[3] What often escapes notice, even by Marx, is how absolute this self-estrangement has become. All our attempts to transcend it in theory only thicken the texture of its apparent totality. Some have searched for a reliable foundation for critique through introspection, thinking that this would ground human beings outside of any of their interactions. Some have posited a foundation outside introspection but within the natural or social world, some call for the conscious creation of a new, arbitrary but usable foundation, and others conclude that there is nothing to be gained from thought but a recognition that thought inevitably pretends to truths that it cannot deliver. The entire progression of romanticism, scientism (including the "science of society" in Engels and Lenin), modernism, and postmodernism seems to follow from this separation, and because all these positions begin from the opposition between individual and social none can find a way out of that split.

It is most likely foolish to expect a discursive way out of a difficulty that was created in part by the assumption that the world could be embraced in discourse. But our self-identification with thinking and our consequent separation from the subpersonal is so entrenched in the way we experience our lives that we know no other way to try. Like the unfortunate prisoner in Villiers de l'Isle-Adam's story "Torture through Hope," though, we find that our attempts at escape simply reinforce our incarceration in the prison of split experience.

We are alone with our projects, then, confronting the world we made and continue to make as if it were an alien power that reduces us to nothing, embroiled in a self-contradictory and self-defeating process that simultaneously severs us from experience and offers us substitutes of which we need ever greater doses. As a replacement for living thought is just as addictive as shopping, and it, too, produces only "enriched privation." Along that path lies only a Malthusian famine, but of words instead of wheat.

Are we thus condemned to live out the consequences of this process, powerless because we have so mystified our own existence that we can no longer act to change it? If discourse cannot remove us from this bind, can it at least open up some possibilities for transformative common life? Perhaps; but the dangers need to be fully appreciated. How deeply and intimately the world of liberal capitalism is woven together with the separation of self and society, of thought and object, is something we have only begun to explore. It is false confidence to think that we can arrive at a solution before living with the problem for a long time, and any license to do so granted by our faith in the discursive grasping of an ordered world should be revoked. We cannot act for the sake of action, but neither can we look back to see what we are bringing into being, hoping to learn how we should act in the future and how the world should run, or like Orpheus turning back at Eurydice we will kill what we value most. It is not an insoluble dilemma, but none of the solutions is simple.

8. A STATE OF SUSPENDED DISINTEGRATION

SOMETHING TERRIBLY IMPORTANT happened in Europe some time between the sixteenth and nineteenth centuries. This is hardly a new insight, but the main points can bear yet another repetition, because it is still difficult for most Westerners to recognize just how backwards Europe was until a few hundred years ago. Ming China was probably the most advanced state of its time, and even after the plagues, civil insurrections, and Manchu conquest of the mid-seventeenth century its successor under the first few Qing emperors was prosperous, artistically creative, and technologically sophisticated. Its peasantry had the highest standard of living anywhere and benefited from the most efficient and thorough system of famine and disaster relief the premodern world was to know. The Ottoman sultans presided over a society more splendid and cultured than any to be found in the petty, warring states of Western Europe, and the merchant centers and textile-producing regions of India were, if anything, even more wealthy. The African kingdoms, though fragmented, would trade as equals with the Portuguese and Dutch until the nineteenth century, and on the other side of the Atlantic, in a world new to Europeans, the Aztecs and Incas built empires and cities that struck their conquerors with awe.

The collapse of Mexico before the horsemen of Cortés and his local allies was the first of an extraordinary series of European triumphs that accelerated to encompass Asia in the eighteenth century and Africa in the nineteenth. Four hundred years after Cortés the 2,100-year-old Chinese empire, all but dismembered by Western gunboats and armies, had vanished in a revolution led by Western-inspired Chinese patriots. Defeat in the First World War put the Ottoman Empire out of its miserable twilight as "the sick man of Europe," and a new Turkish state on European lines emerged under Atatürk, the most successful of all twentieth-century dictators. In Persia the shah of shahs was forced to accept a European-style constitution, in Mexico the postcolonial order was transformed through decades of revolutionary turmoil, and in Japan a campaign of westernization from above turned a minor state with few resources into a direct competitor of the great powers. This list could easily be extended.

We should also remember that most of these changes were concentrated into a period of a little more than a century. Eurocentric historians keep pushing the rise of capitalism farther and farther into the past, but even as late as 1750 Europe, though no longer the backwater it had been at the time of Columbus, was not more economically modern or more developed than Qing China or Tokugawa Japan.

A hundred and twenty years later the situation was completely reversed. Much of the West had entered a second industrial revolution centered on steel and chemicals, and by the beginning of the twentieth century the West provided the only model for modernity. Its prestige and appeal admittedly depended as much on military prowess as on any less intimidating accomplishment. The sheer productivity of the Western economies dwarfed anything the rest of the world could maintain and made possible the vast investment in arms and military adventurism that led to the subjection of most of the globe to European and American colonialism, direct or indirect. The only way to compete, indeed the only way to survive, was to follow the path blazed by the colonial powers.

All the same, the transformations in the West carried their own persuasive power. Europe and the United States increasingly produced the goods that the rest of the world bought, and after the middle of the nineteenth century they did not find it necessary to resort to anything as overt as the Opium Wars to build foreign markets. Technological advances and scientific discoveries filled the pages of a periodical literature bought and read avidly by a newly literate mass public. Living standards rose to an extraordinary degree among the wealthy and the growing middle classes; even among the working class, life expectancy increased in the last decades of the nineteenth century, as public health finally improved in the cities of the industrialized West. The very real obstacles to social mobility should not blind us to the number of "new men" who now occupied the commanding heights of the economic, political, social, and cultural worlds of Europe and the United States. For westernized professionals in the non-Western world, people both highly educated and excluded from power, the ideology of a career open to talents had a particularly strong appeal.

From the European perspective these dizzying changes were proof of the superiority of the Western tradition. This was something new. It went beyond mere ethnocentrism, a bias to which nobody is immune; the Chinese, after all, continue to refer to their country as the Central Kingdom. As inheritors of Rome and as believers in the one true faith Europeans had long felt just as superior as everyone else. The perfection of their institutions and material culture, though, was less obvious and was often doubted. The philosophes of the Enlightenment, assuming the guise of Montesquieu's imaginary Persians or the scarcely less imaginary philosopher-kings that Voltaire saw in the Chinese emperors, took pleasure in mocking their compatriots' self-satisfaction.

By the nineteenth century, though, Persians and Chinese philosophers had begun to appear threadbare if not quaint. European supremacy in arms, science, economic productivity, and cultural accomplishment became the touchstone for all nations. Two points define a line, and as soon as Europeans decided that they lived in the most advanced of societies they endowed history with a course and direction. This set up a race from the past to the present in which Europe came in first by definition. European history became universal history.

It did not seem parochial to Hegel to trace the movement of universal Spirit to his very doorstep, where it occupied itself with the Battle of Jena outside and his composition of the *Phenomenology* within. The universal Spirit had not made extensive use of the history of China, the Ottoman Turks, the Mandan, or the Maori, but Hegel made the generous assumption that, its job having been done in the neighborhood of Prussia, it would move on to bring the rest of the world up to those enlightened standards.

Marx's claim to discover the laws of universal history was fully in this tradition. He may have turned the dialectic on its head, and he certainly had no use for his predecessor's eventual veneration of the Prussian state bureaucracy. But his vision of history presented the European cultural and economic system of the mid-nineteenth-century as a necessary stage for all societies. If history did not conclude with Hegel and Jena, it nonetheless moved inexorably to and through those points on its way to something better.

Marx was nothing if not a universalist. "The history of *all hitherto existing societies*," says the *Communist Manifesto*, "is the history of class struggle" (my italics). In 1853 he wrote that colonial rule in India, however "sickening" and devastating, was to the Indians' eventual benefit, since it destroyed the static system of oriental despotism that blocked their development toward communism.[1] (Twenty-five years later, no longer protected by the static oriental despotism that the British had destroyed, some seven million Indians died of hunger because they could no longer afford food.) The dialectic of historical materialism was in practice as erratic as Hegel's universal Spirit, and left quite as many nations in earlier stages of progress while it was occupied with Europe. Like that Spirit, though, it was an explanation for all that had happened or would happen everywhere.

That all societies are bound to follow the same course of development seems like a bizarre assumption. It is especially odd for Marx, because he insists repeatedly on the conditioned status of so-called human nature. Indeed, the revolutionary thrust of his theory rests on a transformation in consciousness to be brought about through the triumph of the proletariat. Yet this refreshing openness to the possibility that humans might in fact see themselves and relate to each other differently in different cultures is severely limited by Marx's vision of life before the revolution—what he calls prehistory. For in prehistory, which is all we have known to this day, there has been no fundamental change in consciousness. Even though Marx pays lip service to other motives, the isolated, acquisitive, competitive *Homo economicus* of the nineteenth century turns out to be the inhabitant of the vast majority of hitherto existing societies.

Europe's sudden rise to world domination seemed unprecedented to nineteenth-century observers, and it very likely was. The emergence of industrial capitalism, the major contributor to that process, was also unparalleled. Yet Marx and many other historians of both left and right took it to be a universal and necessary phenomenon. One day it may be shown to be this, but so far the evidence for the proposition doesn't exist. Nor has it proved to be a useful tool in analyzing other events. In the People's Republic of China it is, at last, no longer necessary to describe the centralized bureaucratic Imperial state as "feudal." The Marxist historian Ellen Meiksins-Wood has done as much as anyone else to demolish the idea that Athens in the Periclean period can be considered a slave economy, or indeed anything else that would generate contradictions propelling the state toward feudalism. Neither the end of the Roman Empire in the West nor the collapse of the Roman slave economy everywhere was a transitional event that can be explained in terms of internal conflict generating a new social form. Even Marx's understanding of the French Revolution as a bourgeois revolution, indeed the paradigmatic bourgeois revolution, has been shown by George Comninel to have been a cliché of liberal historians, which is substantially undercut by Marx's mature critique.

As the master key to history Marxist analysis raises more false problems than it answers real ones. So important and prestigious have Marxism and its Hegelian predecessors been in defining the discipline's direction, though, that even modern historians, who keep their distance from anything that suggests universal history, continue to argue over insoluble and fruitless questions such as what internal characteristics led the West to develop capitalism while other regions did not.

Merely asking this question assumes that there was something in Western culture—ideological, religious, sociological, economic—that brought about the industrial revolution and the emergence of capitalist modernity. But this, too, needs to be proved instead of assumed, and the proof is lacking. Anthropologist Jack Goody has devoted much of a productive and wide-ranging career to demonstrating that this is a pseudo-problem. Family structure, legal codes, religious traditions, literacy—there was no convincing distinction between "the West and the rest" until the changes that led to the modern industrial state were well underway.

As the engineer and writer Henry Petrosky often points out, success is unilluminating; only failure provides lessons. Nothing can be deduced from the mere fact that Europe got there first, and comparative studies are crippled by the fact that if there were independent processes leading toward a condition resembling modernity none survived European conquest. As we have seen, Europe's rise was sudden and unexpected, and it accelerated as the Western powers were already extending their control to the rest of the world. Internal developments in other regions were aborted by foreign intervention, which destroyed any chance we might have had to see if these cultures would have been able to grow into differently structured societies with living standards and productivity comparable to our own.

It may well be that external rather than internal factors account for the difference. In *The Great Divergence* the economic historian Kenneth Pomeranz has argued that Europe's development after 1750 was made possible only by the easy availability of coal, the surplus from the colonies (especially the slave plantations) and their captive markets, and the wide range of raw materials imported from North America. (Coal is particularly important because it allowed energy-intensive industries to grow beyond the limits imposed by available wood for fuel and spared Europe the disaster of deforestation.) Without these advantages Europe would have been caught in the same Malthusian trap of rising population and limited arable land that halted growth in both China and India.

Pomeranz's thesis suggests another thought, one worth pursuing whatever the merits of his specific argument: that industrialization might not have occurred at all. Technological sophistication, good government, investments in restoring the agricultural environment, and labor-intensive farming can maintain a high population but will eventually lead to a developmental cul-de-sac. This is what happened in China, Japan, and even Denmark. There seems to be no historical inevitability to the emergence of industrial capitalism and Europe was no more prepared for it than anywhere else. Marxian grand narratives and the sociologies of the "West and the rest" have been proposed to explain how the precapitalist European past led to the industrial revolution, but the notion that such a causal connection exists is an unsupported assumption, nothing more.

As Emerson famously remarked, "in analyzing history, do not be too profound; for often the causes are quite superficial." Ascribing European predominance to its culture or social structure has produced little in the way of useful analysis and a good deal of covert ethnocentric self-congratulation—Louis XIV was the Sun King but the Emperor Kangxi was just another oriental despot. It is time to put this question aside. It may be that nothing in the social structure of Western Europe would have led to industrial expansion if the world's coal had been found in China or India instead.

Such speculations can lead us astray too easily. There is insufficient evidence to support or disprove the notion that European culture was innately more capable than any other of a transformation to a condition of high productivity, technological innovation, rising living standards, increased life expectancy, and political stability, all sustainable at least in the middle term. There are experiments that history declines to run for our benefit, and in the absence of such evidence it is better to pose no hypotheses.

This is not to say that the culture of modernity is not itself distinct and worthy of analysis, or that one cannot draw comparisons between the intellectual and ideological forms common under Western capitalism and those of various precapitalist societies. These are very different questions that demand different and much less problematic methodologies, and here Marx's analysis of the social aspects of capitalist production retains most of its force.

Marx's attempt to place economic life at the heart of every society may have been an error, but as an insight into the world of liberal capitalism it can hardly be bettered. Debord, for one, refused to model his hoped-for revolution on the historical triumph of the bourgeoisie and criticized Marxists for their failure to see "the fact that the bourgeoisie is the only revolutionary class that has ever been victorious."[2] But while rejecting both the Jacobinism of the Leninist revolutionary model and the scientism into which Marx gradually declined, he continued to use Marxian concepts as his analytical framework for understanding the present.

There is much to explain. The modernity of the West may have been imposed at first by gunboats and the Maxim gun, but it now exists as a global culture. One does not need to take up the cultural attitudes of Victorian England to see the astonishing and rapid expansion throughout the industrialized world of the basics of the contemporary Western way of life—a modestly regulated corporate capitalism, liberal democracy, the analysis of nature through the "hard" sciences, a nominally free mass media, audience-supported entertainment, universal basic education with status-enhancing higher learning, de jure sexual equality (and de facto inequality), single-generation family structures created by affective instead of arranged marriages, strong parental commitment to child rearing, and a deference to individual choices in love, career, political standpoint, and style of life. Substantial cultural variations do exist even in the most westernized countries, especially in rural areas and among the urban poor; but there, too, the appeal of mainstream Western culture is strong, spread by American film and popular music or local cultural products influenced by American models.

It is not only the international airports that are hard to distinguish one from another; the world's major cities are increasingly similar. Economic globalization is running ahead of cultural globalization, but there is an accelerating convergence of industrialized cultures, and the form on which they are converging is that of the West. (For the moment we must put to one side the different issues raised by economic and social crises in much of the Islamic world and the disasters of postcolonial Africa.)

The most striking aspect of this globalization is that it has taken place with the enthusiastic participation of many of those being westernized, not just the disaffected literati but the mass public. There was more popular resistance to industrialization in England in the eighteenth century than there has been to westernization in most of Asia. There are any number of explanations for this. The modernizing process has recently been somewhat kinder than the spread of the "dark Satanic mills" of Birmingham and Manchester, and—thanks largely to the intervening years of European domination—the immediate premodern conditions were far worse. The apparatus of capitalism has matured and can now be implanted and extended with a minimum of false starts and missteps, and its promotional machinery has been perfected; the apparent ease and comfort capitalism offers are persuasively modeled in the films, television shows and music that dominate the world's media culture.

But there is another, deeper, reason for the ease with which Western ideas and structures have spread. There is a kind of openness to the institutions of the West, an invitation to inhabit them as if they were self-evidently suited for all, that is substantially different from the particularist institutions that they have replaced.

Expensive boutiques in New York sell clothes bearing a French name designed by a Japanese couturier. A South American orchestra performs Beethoven under an Indian conductor with a Korean violinist as soloist, and there is no sense of anyone playing at a borrowed tradition. Uzbeks drink Coke and form hip-hop groups. The secret ballot is adopted everywhere, even if only as a public relations exercise. Everyone wears suits. A popular Chinese film—and a good one—shows its young characters in a Beijing completely devoid of specifically Chinese elements; turn off the sound and aside from the signs its apartment blocks, subway stations, TV news breaks, coffee bars, and Italian restaurants could be anywhere in the world. Why is the intellectual and cultural world of capitalism so easily exported?

Pomeranz's idea that Europe's "take off" after 1750 was the result of fortuitous economic advantages suggests a solution. Industrialization in the eighteenth and nineteenth centuries was disruptive and chaotic, and nobody appeared to be prepared for it. A new class of wealthy entrepreneurs grew rapidly in the industrializing East Midlands and the Northwest while aristocratic fortunes rose and fell with disorienting speed. Even more confusing and far more harrowing was the experience of the majority of English families. What little security one might achieve could be taken away in a moment, with destitution and shame as a result; after his father was imprisoned for debt the young Charles Dickens was forced to work in a shoe-polish factory, and the memory of that horror recurs throughout his novels. The enclosures and consequent evictions, the collapse of traditional cottage industries, the impoverishment of millions of agricultural and proto-industrial workers and their families; mass migrations to slums like those Engels described in *The Condition of the Working Class in England*, epidemics of cholera and gin, the industrialization of prostitution along with production, naked women and children harnessed to carts in the coal mines like donkeys—all this was disorienting and terrifying. The fact that it seemed to come upon a population by surprise would have made a horrible process even worse.

Some took refuge in religion or apocalyptic myth. The character of the English working class owes a great deal to the Wesleys, and the nonconforming chapels played a major role in building a sense of community among those displaced by industrialization. For many even Methodism was an insufficient answer to the dislocations and terrors of the age; the Mormons' heady compound of religious millenarianism and economic and sexual socialism drew many converts from Liverpool and other English industrial cities.

The liberal capitalist world appeared in this period of intense social disorder. But it did not put forth a new order to replace the old one. It was not so much a social form as it was a system that held the human world in a state of suspended disintegration. It seemed to admit and subsume elements of the preceding order, but it allowed them in only to render them meaningless.

The new world dictates no specific "lifestyle" and adheres to no maxims or overt theories of human nature, so it makes little or no difference what form of culture preceded it in any society. It is enough that whatever ties there were between people have weakened to the point of breaking. This social space becomes the necessary and sufficient foundation for the separation imposed by the capitalist order.

This is the reason that liberal capitalism is at home everywhere. It does not reestablish community on other, possibly contentious bases but simply stabilizes whatever process of dissolution is already underway. The solidified fragments of prior life are then represented to us through an unstoppable torrent of discourse and imagery, as in Debord's spectacle.

Capitalism is open to colorful remnants of other practices as long as they are reduced to purely private interests. In the United States, as Will Herberg noted decades ago, social life in ethnic communities became a matter of individual religious identification. Elsewhere—and in some of the remaining aboriginal communities in North America—indigenous cultures are preserved as Disneyfied remnants and marketed to tourists. Though Arab television shows different images of the recent American invasion of Iraq from the ones shown in the United States, their presentation is identical: fast cuts and dissolves among images and graphics, which pass war coverage off as entertainment, extravagant computer-generated network identifiers,

theme music that cues emotional responses, and young, well-mani-
cured news presenters chosen to encourage audience identification.
For all their differences in overt content both al-Jazeerah and
CNN are merely elements in the Debordian spectacle, that common
form which has a more profound impact on life in the modern world
than anything the anchors and analysts actually say:

> Images detached from every aspect of life merge into a com-
> mon stream, and the former unity of life is lost forever.
> Apprehended in a partial way, reality unfolds in a new gener-
> ality as a pseudo-world apart, solely as an object of contem-
> plation. The tendency toward the specialization of images-of-
> the-world finds its highest expression in the world of the
> spectacle, where deceit deceives itself. The spectacle in its
> generality is a concrete inversion of life, and, as such, the
> autonomous movement of non-life.[3]

And what is most crucial in the spectacle is the way it reproduces the
illusion of a purely private individual essence confronting an alien
world outside. This split between the isolated observer and an external social world that is beyond conscious direction, offered "solely
as an object of contemplation," is the key structural element in the
Western world and the solvent with which it dissolves all other ties.
It has become a global condition.

The immediate cause of the globalization of spectacular culture
is the globalization of industrial capitalism. Marx understood that
the reduction of all workers to their individual labor power under
capitalism led to the delusional separation of human beings from
the transformative life of the body:

> Estranged labor therefore turns man's species-being—both
> nature and his intellectual species-powers—into a being alien
> to him and a means of his individual existence. It estranges man
> from his own body, from nature as it exists outside him, from
> his spiritual essence, his human essence.

> An immediate consequence of man's estrangement from the
> product of his labor, his life activity, his species-being, is the
> *estrangement of man from man*....
>
> In general, the proposition that man is estranged from his
> species-being means that each man is estranged from the
> others and that all are estranged from man's essence.
>
> Man's estrangement, like all relationships of man to him-
> self, is realized and expressed only in man's relationship to
> other men.[4]

Capitalism does not and cannot abolish the actual processes of human
self-constitution, the embodied dialogue through which we bring
forth and maintain the world. It merely renders that process opaque
by sustaining a form of experience in which each isolated consciousness confronts the incomprehensible demands of a foreign world:

> I, a stranger, and afraid,
> In a world I never made.

(Similarly, Marx does not argue that "man's species-being" has been
abolished, only that we are estranged from it.)

The role in which one participates in the economic life of capitalism
is always that of a self-sufficient entity facing a separated power in the
form of a market: a job market or a market of commodities or a political
marketplace, even a marketplace of ideas. In every case the actual social
process that generates and sustains people and factories, apartment
blocks, subway systems, political parties, and television news channels
alike is concealed behind a purported rationality of institutions on the
one hand and an even more specious faculty of choice on the part of the
individual, who offers herself freely as a job applicant and who makes
free decisions among alternatives as a consumer or voter.

This is another key to the extraordinary universal power of liberal
capitalist modernity. Prior forms of human life have been sustained

by overt argument, by the authority of myth or religious suasion, by maxims and by force; and myth can be doubted, religious doctrines disputed or disproved, maxims mocked and the brave can challenge the army. But capitalism is different. Its ideology takes the form of experience itself.

The primacy of the individual thinking being—the isolated consciousness to which is ascribed the mystery of free will and the spurious power of free choice—is not a formal proposition for us in the West. It is the character of experience itself. It is the way we live and the way we see ourselves.

This is clearly not the way every culture shapes experience. Writing from a Freudian perspective, the Indian psychoanalyst Sudhir Kakar observes:

> Indian social organization traditionally "took care" of the individual's adaptation to the outer world. That is, traditionally, in the early years, the mother serves as the child's ego, mediating his most elementary experiences, well into the years of childhood proper, until around the age of four. The ego's responsibility for monitoring and integrating reality is then transferred from the mother to the family-at-large and other social institutions. Thus, while making decisions based on reasoning through the pros and cons of a situation, the individual functions as a member of a group rather than on his own.[5]

The long precolonial history of Indian economic innovation and social change shows that this character type is fully compatible with a high level of technology and development. Yet it may well be that Europe's specific intellectual resources left it better able to imagine and cope with the experience of life in a world restructured by industrial capitalism. The experiential world of capitalism (though not its real structure) coheres well with the primacy long given rational discourse and instrumental reason in the West, and historically it can be made to look like a natural development of the privatization of religious experience inherent in Western Christianity especially, reinforced by the primacy of doctrine in the way the barbarian kingdoms were Christianized and ultimately triumphant in the development of Protestantism a millennium later.

But even if the Western tradition is uniquely suited to the demands of capitalist modernity, its global success comes not from any intellectual superiority but from its economic domination of the rest of the world. The spectacle and its atomized viewers are a global phenomenon simply because there is virtually no place in which the ties of culture have not been eroded by the corrosive effects of the market.

And the liberal capitalist order, as ever, stands ready to provide a solution. The world no longer works. Our expectations are frustrated. Philosophy, law, medicine, and theology only show the impossibility of knowledge. The future cannot be predicted and chaos looms. At this crisis point capitalism steps forward like Mephistopheles in Faust. It promises the satisfaction of all legitimate desires: freedom and plenty, dignity and respect, pluralism and democracy—an alluring sales pitch when everything solid has melted into air. It proclaims a zone of privacy for each person; we can cultivate whatever kind of life we want that doesn't harm someone else. The only thing it requests is a separation between the personal and the social. A small thing, perhaps, but as soon as it is granted we find ourselves in a regime of mediated experience, stunted creativity channeled into acquisitive materialism, and political vacuity.

This accounts for the rootless, static quality of life under capitalism. Within the presuppositions of the liberal order effective opposition vanishes. The fragmentation and antagonistic character of life is obvious, but it cannot be challenged by those who argue that the contemporary world gives too little emphasis to social needs. Since these critics begin from the same starting point as everyone else. they can come up with no justification for community except individual benefit. Social life becomes either a combination for goals which are determined outside of or prior to joining the community or a kind of ethical taxation whereby we give up a certain portion of our independence to receive a service we could not provide for ourselves.

This failure is inevitable, because the split between individual and social rests on the deeper schism between bodily and conscious experience itself. It is a rupture in our hearts, a split that runs through each of us and cuts us off from our corporeal selves. We no longer acknowledge the thought of the body, through which all of us together generate and recreate our selves and our worlds. Identifying ourselves with our conscious existence alone, we are driven further and further within, seeking a "true" nature unsullied by the demands of the world. To act out of anything else is conformism, a loss of individuality and authenticity, a kind of betrayal. We watch ourselves carefully and others even more.

But to be left with nothing but conscious reflective activity is to be awarded the booby prize. The actual public processes of our bodily cognition are now ranged against us as in the guise of the social world. Though they are as much our own activity as anything we say to ourselves in private, they manifest themselves within—if they show up at all—as irrational urges, threats to our well-laid plans, voices of the profane world, alien invaders. And as we identify ourselves with the shrinking and increasingly barren territory within which we can pretend to exercise true autonomy, the same separation between individual and social worlds leaves us powerless to change anything in the sphere of the social. We are free but impotent.

The social world and its discourse have all the prestige of the certain and the rational. They claim to impose no standard and to have no function except to guarantee that nobody passes judgment on our inner lives, and once we accept the separation of self and other we cannot say or do anything that will shake these claims—There Is No Alternative. To criticize them from the standpoint of individual choice or happiness courts incoherence. Any opposition to these institutions inevitably appears as an attack on the freedom they protect. Indeed, those who begin from liberal presuppositions and then delude themselves into thinking that they have transcended the specific forms of capitalism have time and again created horrors that never deliver the promised transformation of humanity. They do nothing but eliminate what little actually remains of the dignity and freedom that liberal capitalism promises. The police states of vanguard socialism suffered from all of capitalism's contradictions and added their own more oppressive lies to the mix.

The apparent freedom we have in private thus comes with a high price. I am nominally free to do anything; the only exception is that I have no right to speak for anyone other than myself. Language has lost the power to say "we."

A professor of mine once said that under capitalism you could say whatever you liked, so long as it didn't make a difference. He might better have said that you can say whatever you like *because* it will make no difference. Capitalism embraces discourse, but it does so only because what we say no longer points outside itself. In a world of totalizing discourse any glimpse of genuine life lies outside language and thus appears nonsensical or chaotic. Discourse has lost the mystified referent it used to have in the religious sphere, which is now isolated from the economic, social, and political worlds, and the real world of bodily transformation outside of consciousness that it used to evoke has thus vanished from sight. The only job left to language is maintaining the fiction that nothing else matters. It is at once universal and empty.

The vaunted pluralism of the modern capitalist world neither stigmatizes social expression nor allows it to be effective. It tolerates and makes use of political and social conflict, transgressive art, sexual and transsexual variety, and every manner of specious diversity. All these can be merchandised, but their usefulness goes well beyond than their market value. They contribute to the thick texture of discourse in which we confine ourselves. Political and social debates are endless by their very nature; they function not to resolve anything but to reinforce the unspoken presuppositions shared by both parties. Their starting point is the separation between people and they do nothing but reproduce that separation.

This is the true social function of cultural activity in our world. We think our feet are firmly planted on the ground, but instead we walk on the glittering cloth of the spectacle, cloth woven from discourse that enshrines the false dichotomies of the capitalist world.

In the silencing of the body, the space between discourse and experience that allows creativity and spontaneity to flourish has collapsed. We cover over this wound with useless words. Among them are the slogans that only in this way is human freedom genuinely protected and that capitalism is therefore the sole guardian of universal human values. But capitalist modernity can lay legitimate claim to one kind of universality only: it is the universal imposition of human isolation and the obliteration of spontaneity and individuality.

The disruption and horror of rapid industrialization might have happened elsewhere. It might have then taken different form and created different social patterns. It did not, of course. If there is no reason to believe that the European past furnished the tools for creating the modern industrial economy, there are good reasons to argue that it supplied the framework for the specific form that this world took in the nineteenth century and later, and that it was well suited to forging modern liberal capitalism into the basis of a global culture. The inner focus of Christianity, the belief in the human ability to arrive at unassailable certainty, and the primacy of rational discourse—all these fit well with the linked schisms in experience that make possible the uniquely rooted structure of experience under capitalism. In our response to the chaos of industrialization we built a form of life that appears to embrace all the past and all human ways, and which renders them all equally meaningless. That is our gift to the world.

9. POLITICS WITHOUT GOALS

A SPECTER HAUNTS THE WEST, a dream of clarity and purity, of freedom and painlessness in which all the tears of earthly life are bathed away: a new and different world that we inherit in heaven or can build here on this green and pleasant land. In Bergman's *Seventh Seal* the guileless Jof sees it as Death leads away most of the other admirable but much-less-innocent characters of the film. And for Jof, as for us, seeing is knowing. In our tradition the transcendent is something that is seen and the wished-for gift is perfect sight and thus perfect knowledge. "I once was blind," goes the song, "but now can see." "Now we see as through a glass, darkly," said Paul, "but then, face to face."

Adam gave the animals their true names, those that corresponded to their god-given natures, and we may presume that he was able to do this spontaneously; the legend is that he "spoke without hesitation,"[1] because in the pure light of the Garden of Eden one had only to look to see the truth of things. Indeed,

> [t]he celestial light, whereby Adam could survey the world
> from end to end ... was but one of seven precious gifts
> enjoyed by Adam before the fall and to be granted to man
> again only in the Messianic time.[2]

After the theophany on Sinai Moses was so imbued with the celestial light—the *shekinah*—that he had to veil his face so its glow would not blind the Israelites. It is that same light, fragmented and buried in countless places, that the Kabbalist seeks to gather together once more to restore creation to its Adamic splendor.

The warm sun of a perfect world bathes the imaginary Netherlands of Baudelaire's "L'invitation au voyage:"

> Le monde s'endort
> Dans une chaude lumière!

> Là, tout n'est qu'ordre et beauté,
> Luxe, calme et volupté.

Yeats conjured it in "the holy of Byzantium," where he could be gathered into "the artifice of eternity." But it has also been claimed by the revolutionary movements of the West.

This should not be a surprise. Many of the great uprisings of the early modern period hoped to build god's kingdom on earth. The peasant movements that so disturbed Luther were often explicitly apocalyptic, sharing the hopeful belief of the twelfth-century mystic Joachim of Fiore that the holy spirit had already been poured out and the new world was about to appear. Apocalyptic and millenarian hopes attended the English Civil War in the 1640s, and not merely in the radical fringe of Diggers and Quakers. Similar dreams inspired the Puritans who had fled to make a fresh start in a *new* England. Millenarian speculation played a prominent role in the intellectual background of the American revolution more than a century later, and it remains an important if little-acknowledged strain in American thought.

The tendency of even modern revolutionary thought to converge on or occupy the territory of messianic religion is so obvious that it has become a conservative cliché. It is a temptingly easy way to discredit any serious attempt to change or criticize the present state of things; the gruesome results of the institutionalized utopias of Russian communism and the varied European fascisms are now so obvious that we fear anything that even hints at a social transformation. Yet the dream of perfect knowledge survives in our tradition's drive toward the perfect congruence of the subject of consciousness with the subject of action, through closure in theory and art and in the conscious myth of an infinitely deferred future that some hope will illuminate the limitations of the present.

But what could it mean to experience the redemption of discourse, the restoration of Adamic speech in which words and things are identical, where to speak is to speak truth, where our thoughts grasp reality in all its fullness? What would it be like to live in a truly thinkable world?

We have no way of imagining this. No road leads from here to there. No art known can light the world with another sun; our dreams, like birds, take flight from and return to the soil of the only earth we can know, and the only judgment they can pass on our lives are internal ones. Our longing for transparency, purity, freedom, and truth can shape our arts, but longing cannot bring us those dubious gifts any more than the fear of death can prove the existence of an afterlife. And would it not be better, after all, to be free from "that vision which forever compels us to evaluate our acts in the light of imaginary criteria transcending the situation in the midst of which, here and now, we act"?[3]

Art and all other forms of creativity arise in the unspeakable space between discourse and the subpersonal thought of the body. But their function is to naturalize that space, to render it knowable from within the common world; otherwise they slip into solipsism, incoherence, or the merely private. The implied critique of a work of art must be generated within the culture's own conversation. Criticism may speak from the margins of discourse, but without such boundaries it could not work. And margins exist only because a culture has staked out some territory as its own.

Why, then, the persistence of these hopes? "All desire craves eternity," as Nietzsche says; but a life circumscribed by the limits of conscious discourse is an additional trial, as so much of our most deeply human activity appears to us as the demands of an alienated social realm. Since we cannot see through the illusion of our separation, we look to an equally illusory future state in which each of us is granted an individual reconciliation with the social. The dream of transcendental knowledge leaves the split between personal and social in place, but it offers the comforting notion that we are foreigners to this flawed world. It says, consolingly, that the life in which we are embraided is somehow alien to us, but it has been foisted on us and needs only to be shaken off; history is a nightmare from which we can awake into the state for which we were intended.

But each of us will wait outside the door, the one intended for nobody else, until it is closed at our death. We are social beings throughout, not preexisting individuals socialized into an equally preexistent social order; everything about us and our world is found in the way we perceive and act within it—experience consists in nothing else, after all. Like it or not, this is the world we have made. There is no way out and nowhere else we can go.

Nor are we free at any level from the taint of our culture's flaws. Power is not secured through fear and cannot long be maintained by the barrel of a gun. It does indeed rest largely on consensus, borne not just through discourse but in the shapes of the subpersonal activity through which we make ourselves and each other. Our own common acts are the very vehicle of domination, the process whereby unequal relations are recreated and become second nature. Coal miners may no longer fumble with their caps and stare at the ground when addressing their "betters," but the horrible, unthinking deference of the working class survives, in the opacity with which the world seems to present itself to the poor, a reluctance to question doctors, lawyers, and bureaucrats or even to ask for an explanation, or simply a persistent sense of unease—all of which can explode into blind, self-destructive rage. Oppression is learned exactly the way a dog learns to cringe. I.L. Peretz's Bontshe the Silent, who had never grasped his own strength, could not undo a life of submission; when offered any boon that heaven could give he asked, to shamed silence from the angels and the prosecutor's mocking laughter, for a hot roll and butter every morning for breakfast.

But it was Bontshe's and is our world, and we make it along with everyone else. People certainly suffer within it, but this does not mean that the machinery of oppression can be teased apart from the process whereby we make our lives. We cannot extricate ourselves whole from the sorrows of the world, any more than we would be the same person if we had been born to different parents. Nor can we view it from the outside—there is no outside to it, just as there is no outside to the physical universe, not even emptiness. The oppressed have no better perspective on the realities of our activity than the oppressors, only the constant reminder that something is indeed wrong.

Dreaming has always had a political function. It provides a kind of safety valve for the inevitable inconsistencies and sorrows of life. But it also discharges some of the misery caused by that single, all-pervading split on which liberal capitalism rests—the illusion that we can stand aside from social process, that we are self-created or enter our lives with a soul made in some heavenly or sociobiological forgery—which is the very foundation of our economic and social order. With that split comes the eclipse of the communal subject of action and our own powerlessness. Neither art nor the politics of ethnic or sexual identity, which simply replace the specious independence of the individual with the equally false independence of the oppressed as a group, can do anything to relieve this impotent isolation, but they offer to some the illusion or hope of an ultimate reconciliation that makes it easier to bear. For many that promise sustains the myths with which they explain their plight to themselves. Religion still has many adherents, but for today's unbelievers the opiate of choice is theory.

The central legitimating rituals of both representative democracy and market economics base their authority on the separation of the thinking subject, and for that reason they are trapped in the same circularity as the dreams of the discontented. In the voting booth, for example, we leave the world behind. Alone with our conscience, with our dreams of how the world should be, isolated from social pressure—the ballot is secret, after all—and apparently free, we vote from our inmost hearts. The supermarket aisle is the same; the responsible consumer reads the unit prices, the ingredient lists and nutrition charts, and protects herself from the manipulation of unscrupulous advertisers by the information provided and her ability to weigh competing claims rationally.

However useful voting and markets may be for assessing preferences in large groups, they are rituals which do double duty. They appear transparent and value-neutral, mere vehicles that effectuate choices made elsewhere. Liberal theorists of course recognize and decry the manipulation and biases in information that pollute the free and independent choices we think we are making. But politicians cursed with perfect candor and newspapers of godlike detachment would not make us any more independent. Nobody steps outside our world for any purpose. Whether we are in private or in a group certainly affects what we do and think, but one action is no more individual than the other; a lynch mob and the United States Supreme Court are composed of equally social creatures. The benefits of a considered process for collective decision making are obvious; one would in all cases prefer a court to a throng with torches and a noose. What cannot be shown is that any way of assessing preferences has validity outside its own terms.

Elections and market behavior give us only the current state of a system, not the sum of decisions made elsewhere. They can neither justify their results nor transcend the system in which they operate.

These attempts to ground institutions outside of common life only reproduce the fallacious input/output scheme of mental activity. The voting booth, for example, is the macrocosmic equivalent of the black-box mind of the Standard Cognitive Science Model. We take in information from the news media, campaign leaflets, stump speeches, the internet, and kitchen-table gossip. We output our vote. As we have seen, though, action and perception are not separated, and there is no intervening decision-making process in any mental black box. Perception itself is an intersubjective phenomenon, as Husserl discovered. So there is no private space from which we pass judgment on ourselves or our surroundings; our judgments—which are real ones—emerge as moments in an unending unspoken conversation. Seen this way, the walls of the voting booth dissolve and our decisions appear as the social acts that they are.

But if we cannot dream, think, create, or vote ourselves out of this unhappy world, what can we hope to do by way of criticism or politics? In his early years Marx thought he had discovered the answer. His writings of the 1840s reveal a kind of wager: that the emerging industrial proletariat was creating, at least in potential form, a genuinely postcapitalist (one might say postmodern) form of life. The working class could assume this role because it had been completely cut off from social power. It was totally alienated, totally oppressed, and this class with "radical chains" could therefore embody a standpoint that was an equally total negation of alienation and oppression. Its present-day life was not in itself communism, but what it embodied today would be forged into the life of the future through revolutionary struggle, at once social change and self-change—processes, which the struggle would show to be identical. The proletariat would bring to consciousness the true machinery of history, something that had appeared before only in alienated, mystified form.

This is a theory deeply indebted to Hegel, which is at once its strength and its weakness. In *Philosophy and Revolution* Stathis Kouvelakis argues that for the Marx of the early 1840s the proletariat was fundamentally a philosophical entity and a vantage point that revealed the contradictions in bourgeois society, not a group of real people whose misery had been discovered by empirical investigation. (Kouvelakis sees the Engels of the same period as a "social-ist," driven by a concern for the actual conditions of working class life, not unmixed with fear and sexual fascination, to craft a reformed social order in which human needs would be better met.) But Marx's proletariat is more than a mere concept. He needed such an entity to exist in reality instead of theory, because if there were no community that was making present the life of the postcapitalist world there would be no way to project that future simply by thinking. Such a future is literally unimaginable, as Marx explicitly argued in the third of his famous *Theses on Feuerbach*:

> The materialistic teaching on the changing of circumstances and education forgets that the circumstances are changed by men, and it is necessary that the educator himself be educated. This teaching, therefore, is bound to split society into two parts, of which one is superior to the other. The concurrence of changing of the circumstances and of the human activity, or self–changing, can be conceived as *revolutionary practice*.[4]

Marx's point was that self-change and thinking are neither separate from circumstances and human activity nor epiphenomenal. Both are interwoven with each other and mutually dependent; as Nathan Rotenstreich says, Marx's theory forswears any "first foothold" in one side or the other.[5] These aspects have appeared to be separate only because they had previously been addressed in isolation, either objectively as "actuality [or] sensuousness" or subjectively as "as human sensuous activity, [or] practice."[6] "Revolutionary" or "practical-critical activity" is the realization of the unity of these two aspects. ("Realize" should here be understood in both senses.)

It should not be necessary to belabor the clear parallels between this theory of the relationship between thinking and activity and the one advanced in these essays. But there are crucial differences as well. Marx's theory supports a critique of the illusion of separate human subjects; he indicts Feuerbach for a position that can contemplate only "single individuals and civil society" instead of "human society or social humanity."[7] But it adheres to the closely related ideal of conscious transparency, the faith that all human activity can be made rationally knowable. It simply looks to a social process and a future social order instead of to philosophy for the attainment of that rather Hegelian goal. Although Marx, at least in this period, saw the future as a continuous and unpredictable process of revolutionary change—a point Kouvelakis brings out in his magisterial work—he did see the imminent proletarian revolution as the one genuinely transformative act in human history. The revolution would be more than an event in consciousness. It would be the true birth of consciousness; from that point on history would be made knowingly. In other words, conscious rationality, having come into its own, would grasp and henceforth govern all human activity. The celestial light would return.

Hopes such as these could only be disappointed. Marx had achieved only a more plausible form of the same linguistic totalitarianism that has recurred in the West since the Stoics. The transparency and rational comprehension of human activity that were to result from the proletarian revolution could never have been achieved; such projects for deifying humanity fail not because it is sacrilege to aspire to godhead but because no divine vantage point could ever exist. In the words of Jean-Marie Vincent,

> [Marx] overestimated the power of oppressed individuals and groups to throw over cognitive and cultural structures as well as limitations of social practices. This led him to transfigure, virtually to deify, the wage laborer, who even before any process transforming the social relations of labor became the emblematic incarnation of emancipation.[8]

But there was never a working-class revolution in any event, though Lenin and his successors tried to pass off theirs as genuine fulfillments of the Marxian prophecy. In 1848 workers' uprisings spread throughout Western Europe. They were all suppressed. Isolated national revolts, often following defeat in war, kept the revolutionary flame alive for the next seven decades, but by the time a government pledged to Marx's principles achieved lasting power all hint of the self-transforming nature of his early theory had been lost or suppressed—a loss for which Marx, whose response to the failures of

1848 colored his thought for the rest of his life, surely bears some responsibility. It was a difficult argument in any event, and even Engels was unable to grasp the full implications of his friend's work—a failure perhaps exemplified by his decision to remove the words "or self-change" when he first published the *Theses on Feuerbach*. This watering-down left a hole in the center of what remained of Marxism, which was now presented as "the science of society"—just another exercise in thinking, with the usual claims to be the whole truth.

Nor was the twentieth century any kinder to Marx's hopes, though the disappearance of the Soviet Union, a parody Marxist state simultaneously ludicrous, pathetic, and terrifying, was a net gain to theory if not to world stability. Attempts to fill the hole in the center of "scientific" Marxism with Freudianism or another "science of the soul" failed to retain what was valuable and living in Marx's original vision, and the prospects for revolutionary change have receded year by year. The industrial proletariat in the first world has been vanishing for decades and it still shows no signs of achieving the consciousness Marx and Lukács once imputed to it. Even though much of the misery and poverty of a globalized capitalism has now been exported to the third world the workers of those countries seem farther from Marx's proletariat than their first world predecessors ever were. This may be a triumph of ideological misdirection. We may be expecting a cultural transformation in Africa, Asia, and Latin America that has yet to occur. Or it may be that Marx's underlying model was flawed.

It is tempting to leave such theories behind. We are well done with dreams; they all become nightmares in the daylight. And there is certainly enough to occupy ourselves with in the simple amelioration of the condition of the world. At the very least we ought to try to guarantee that a habitable planet will still be around for our children, their children, and even the shareholders of a capitalist future.

Even this modest achievement is unlikely if we let events follow their own logic. Conditions in the industrialized world are still tolerable and even luxurious for a great many, but this prosperity is increasingly unequal in its distribution and looks more and more tenuous. Worse yet, it leaves out and progressively impoverishes at least half of the world's population: billions of people without clean water, sanitation, work of any sort, education, or health care. In much of Africa and Latin America and parts of Central Asia per capita GNP and living standards have been falling since the 1970s. Even without the demographic disaster of the AIDS pandemic and the unpredictable ravages of climate change many third world countries would be moving toward economic collapse. At the same time the industrialized nations, the United States most of all, are exhausting the world's resources at an accelerating rate. If even a sizable fraction of the third world were to consume the way the United States does global energy supplies would be entirely used up in a few years. The head of the U.N.'s environment program has argued that the ambitious economic goals of the People's Republic of China cannot be achieved simply because they demand more resources for their fulfillment than the earth can supply.

This is a volatile situation. Increasing poverty, disease, and instability in many parts of the world, decreasing resources to support the one-sided prosperity of the industrialized world, major global threats such as climate change and possible technological disasters—the "gray goo" horror some critics of nanotechnology fear—none of these is likely to vanish because of some scientific breakthrough. Technological optimists assume that some unforeseeable invention will appear in time to solve every problem we face. Their more detailed projections look disturbingly like the well-known S. Harris cartoon in which a mathematician's blackboard proof contains a step labeled "then a miracle occurs." Humanity, it must be admitted, has pulled off a good many miracles. But the challenges we face are so grave that it would be foolhardy to count on them in every instance.

It does not require any sophisticated social theory to grasp these threats. Indeed, it requires some degree of theoretical commitment—to apocalyptic Christianity, for example—to deny it. Nor should an appeal to altruism be needed to garner support for genuine change. It makes only short-term economic sense to continue to expend a finite resource and create conditions that in just a few decades will measurably depress world productivity.

Yet we do nothing. The need for change may be obvious, but the culture of our age makes the obvious choice seem intolerably painful. Our insatiable demand for control of our lives, the enriched privation that demands to be fed with more and more goods like the all-devouring No-Face of Miyazaki's *Spirited Away*—these feed a spiral of self-destructive consumption. Afraid we are nothing, we want everything. Severed from the ways in which we make ourselves, confronting our own creative power as an alien force that ceaselessly threatens to overwhelm our identities, we are driven to construct worlds of our own in which we can maintain the fragile illusion that we are independent beings.

Like Lévi-Strauss's *bricoleur* we use whatever comes to hand. Our DVD players, Beanie Babies, designer clothes, posters, Hello Kitty paraphernalia, coffee table books, souvenir miniature spoons, motorboats, counted cross-stitch samplers, flags, faux-Tiffany lampshades, computer screen savers, framed diplomas, CD racks, Impressionist or Old Master paintings, knickknack shelves with knickknacks, SUVs, garden gnomes, vials of sand from the Dead Sea, coin collections, and reproduction Chinese furniture give pleasure, but they multiply incessantly because they are also the fragments we shore against the ruins of our common life. This endless hunger feeds the equally endless rapacity of constant economic growth. And the dread of our self-made isolation, the emotional impoverishment of our culture and the resigned belief in our own powerlessness will not change no matter how rational capitalist production becomes or how fair we make international trade.

We seem to be at an impasse. Art shows us only ourselves in a mirror. Revolutionary politics is a mirage or the imposition of a fragmentary understanding of human activity that is mistaken for the whole. We are left with well-meaning liberalism, valuable and perhaps even essential within its limits, but unable to deliver us from the hunger at its heart, from the discontents Freud claimed were the price of civilization. A more human as well as a more equitable life: one in which we recognize ourselves in others, no longer afraid of the transformations of our mutual creativity or driven to construct a world of commodities in which to shelter from the world of commodity production, in which we might live more fully instead of living within ideas of life—have we no path there?

★ ★ ★

At this point, dear reader, I hesitate. I know it is dispiriting to come to the close of a critique and find that the author thinks it necessary to make positive suggestions. Even the least fatuous proposals are disappointing, the way a fictional detective's prosaic explanations deflate the vertiginous and even voluptuous pleasure we had taken in a murder mystery's puzzles. Yet it would seem a greater betrayal of whatever confidence you have invested in these pages for me to leave you with an irresolvable aporia or a despairing dismissal of the future.

I cannot tell you what will come or how you should act; Augustine somewhere says that nobody can say with certainty even what he or she will do tomorrow. But we can and must go forward precisely because modernity presents itself as the end of history and may all too easily make good on that claim. Marx was wrong in his estimation of the potential of the industrial proletariat and wrong, too, in his dream of a world of perfect transparency and light. But he was right in his understanding that a world different from the fragmented totality of the present will be made the same way that this one is: not in theory but by the bodies of people in their lives together. As Vincent summarizes the Marx of the *Grundrisse*, "Self-realization or self-effectuation is as much an individual socialization as it is a socialized individuation; it cannot spring forth from sundered subjectivities, but takes root in new social practices, themselves borne up by new ideas about society and the world."[9] We need to create that common life yet at the same time let it shape itself, the way Mencius talks of the virtues: "You must be willing to work at it, understanding that you cannot have precise control over it. You can't forget about it, but you can't force it to grow, either."[10]

That possibility seems a distant one today. Modernity's elimination of visible community and the concomitant destruction of genuine cultural diversity is as threatening to the future as the loss of biological diversity is to our physical survival. Capitalism may produce its gravediggers, but no historical necessity compels it to bring forth its successor. Nor can we, products and producers of the present, plan or project one.

In spite of this there is a way forward. *One* way, I am tempted to write, though it is a way that encompasses many ways without being bound to any of them. It is a *via negativa*, a negative politics of purposeful action without predetermined goals.

Christians can follow a negative theology because they are assured that an omnipresent deity lies behind all human institutions and thought; these obstructions need only be cleared away to reveal the divine. A negative politics has similar hopes. It is grounded in the fact that our mutual self-constitution continues regardless of the ways in which we construe our experience. It opposes certainties and assurances of knowledge, but not in the name of either a different certainty or of a human characteristic that is presumed to lie beneath the social. It has hopes, not of a world that it already knows how to think about, but of one that will not claim to be the culmination of time and that will not hold to ideas, ideals, or even values that seek to arrest the endless transformations of our lives together. It looks not to the perfection of detached knowledge but to an expanding attentiveness to embodied understanding. It is a path not to the future but to a deeper experience of the present.

Right now we would rather run from such a world. In the West's drive toward certainty, objectivity, and a world grasped in thought, the disappearance of our embodied life appears as a virtue. The deeply ambivalent conclusion to *Tristes Tropiques* rests on this inversion. Lévi-Strauss trys to sketch a path away from "our present serfdom"

[t]he grace to call a halt, that is to say: to check the impulse
which prompts Man always to block up, one after the other,
such fissures as may be open in the blank wall of necessity
and to round off his achievement by slamming shut the doors
of his own prison....On this opportunity, this chance of for once
detaching oneself from the implacable process, life itself depends.[11]

All that is human is soiled by the social, and the sole grace lies in the
inhuman:

the essence of what our species has been and still is, beyond
thought and beneath society ...may be vouchsafed to us in a
mineral more beautiful than any work of Man; in the scent,
more subtly evolved than our books, that lingers in the heart
of a lily; or in the wink of an eye, heavy with patience, serenity, and mutual forgiveness, that sometimes, through an
involuntary understanding, one can exchange with a cat.[12]

It is as if we alone are not part of this world, as if in the eyes of our
lovers we ourselves are not more beautiful, subtly evocative, or for-
giving than anything in the nonhuman world. And for that reason
the only thing Lévi-Strauss can see his way toward is contemplation,
"leisure, and recreation, and freedom, and peace of body and mind."
    We must, instead, try to reopen the doors we have closed,
remembering that the most important kind of human creativity is
not that of the artist but the ceaseless re-creation and transformation
of our common world. The economic processes of capitalism did
not give birth to a postcapitalist form of life and thought. It may now
be time for us to make the attempt, essaying a thousand ways of
building common lives, as in the Warring State period a thousand
schools of thought arose. As Miguel Benasayag and Diego Sztulwark
have written, "The only genuinely serious thing is the construction
of a true anticapitalist revolt, of new solidarities within situations."[13]
Many of them will fail. All of them may fail. But though we should

hold them to the standards of an ethics like that of Mencius and can criticize them and demand that they criticize themselves, we cannot in a deep way prejudge them.

Forms, routines, habits, and degrees of common life: perhaps in worker collectives, here and in the Third World, that one day might become communities, or communities that might one day begin to produce goods, steps pioneered by the Zapatista Autonomous Municipalities and the recuperated factories and micro-enterprises of Argentina after the 2001 collapse; perhaps with origins as bourgeois-seeming as the cohousing communities that started in the 1970s in Denmark—an intriguing example because the most successful groups have created themselves as they planned and built their housing, without persuading themselves that they existed as a community on the basis of theoretical allegiances or political identification. There is much to learn, too, in the history of anarchism, an often-reviled tradition that at its best grasps the unity of self- and social change far better than do the epigones of Marx. Miguel Benasayag has written thoughtfully of those spontaneous, leaderless groups in Latin America and Europe who, like the Zapatistas and the Brazilian landless, lay down their path in walking. Whatever we do, though, we need to attend to our attempts and learn from them. Just as nobody writes without wanting to see what the work itself says, so we must listen to our own histories as we make them. As the Zapatistas have said, "preguntando caminamos"—walking, we question.

A negative politics is not an abstention from life. It should tell us what Rilke heard from the archaic torso of Apollo: that we must change our lives, that we can escape neither the obligation to act nor the obligation to criticize ourselves and the grounds on which we act. In 1843 Marx wrote his friend Ruge, "If we have no business with the construction of the future or with organizing it for all time, there can still be no doubt about the task confronting us at present: the *ruthless criticism of the existing order*, ruthless in that it will shrink neither from its own discoveries, nor from conflict with the powers that be." Since that existing order is ours and is maintained through our own acts and ideas, this can only be a call for a critique which does not shrink from turning on itself.

A negative politics opens us to our world the way the thought of Nagarjuna and Wittgenstein strive to do—thought that is meaningless without action and that indeed restores us to action. It tells us that our ideas about the world are not the world, that we are right to take pleasure from each other, that human warmth, love, and the experience of joy—things not perceived but embodied—are touchstones precisely as they are inadequately grasped in any system of thought, that only the irreducible is true. It opens us to pain, too, and to despair, to tears that cannot be washed away by the wings of angels or the dream of a spotless future. As Nietzsche says in *The Birth of Tragedy*, "All that exists is just and unjust and equally justified in both."[14]

We look back from what we thought was our exile and discover that no angel with a flaming sword bars our way, but that no Eden rises there either. It has always been our world, and we have never been out of it. We should realize that this is not a loss. Neither we nor our most distant descendants will build the New Jerusalem or the Garden of Eden; but we have, if we choose it, the pleasure of clearing the ground, hoping only that one day other hands will cultivate something more like a garden—a flawed and human garden, under sun, clouds, fog, and rain, with our own ants and slugs and weevils but alive with our own raspberry bushes, too, our weeping cherries and roses, our own vines, and our own fig trees.

SUGGESTIONS
FOR FURTHER READING

T HE TOPICS TOUCHED ON HERE are so vast that a comprehensive bibliography might easily be as long as this entire book. I can do nothing more than point to a few starting points that I have found helpful myself.

To begin with autopoietics: There is a great deal of material on this school of theoretical biology on the web, including several important papers by Maturana. This material is most easily accessed through the Observer Web, www.enolagaia.com/AT.html. For print references, one might begin with the thorough exposition of their approach that Maturana and Varela wrote for a nonspecialist audience, *The Tree of Knowledge*; but although this book is both thoughtful and beautifully produced, it lacks the suggestive power and intellectual excitement of their first joint publication, the difficult to find *Autopoiesis and Cognition*. The best compromise is probably *The Embodied Mind*, which Varela wrote with Evan Thompson and Eleanor Rosch, although that work's many parallels with Buddhism would be more convincing if they were not pushed quite so far. Readers should note, too, that Rosch's influential theories on prototyping and concept formation have come in for increasing criticism; for one example see Frank Keil's *Concepts, Kinds and Cognitive Development*.

Varela and Maturana are better known in Europe than in the United States, where cognitive science adheres more strictly to a computationalist paradigm. Of the "mainstream" American cognitive scientists the one whose work combines most interestingly with theirs is Gerald Edelman. He has presented a semi-popular account of his "neural Darwinism" in Bright Air, Brilliant Fire. (I have not had the opportunity to read his latest in this genre, Wider than the Sky.) Those who would like to investigate his approach further may wish to refer to his earlier books listed in the bibliography, which though more specialized are not difficult for lay readers.

The surprisingly limited role that conscious activity plays has received the popular-science treatment in Tor Nørretranders's The User Illusion. Some of the key experiments in this field were performed by Benjamin Libert, and he has presented a useful account of his work in Mind Time. Libert's attempts to draw larger conclusions from his experimental results, though, are unconvincing; a much more coherent and satisfactory analysis, not without its own difficulties, can be found in Daniel Wegner's The Illusion of Conscious Will.

Complementing this research, and fascinating in their own right, are Antonio Damasio's books, especially Descartes' Error, and V. S. Ramachandran and Sandra Blakeslee's Phantoms in the Brain. Ramachandran has stressed elsewhere the importance of the discovery of mirror neurons by the neurologists at the University of Parma. Those who wish to investigate this work further will find a substantial number of papers downloadable from that department's web sites; Giacomo Rizzolatti's page is www.unipr.it/arpa/mirror/english/staff/rizzolat.htm and Vittorio Gallese's is www.unipr.it/arpa/mirror/english/staff/gallese.htm.

One might have hoped that after Richard Lewontin's and Susan Oyama's work the nature/nurture controversy would have been laid to rest for good. This hasn't happened, of course, and their books are still needed. Lewontin has given us a short, non-technical account of his approach in The Triple Helix. Oyama, less prolific, has not, but there is nothing forbidding in either The Ontogeny of Information or Evolution's Eye.

Few academic philosophers have taken up the challenge of this research. Susan Hurley's difficult, uningratiating, but brilliant *Consciousness in Action* does. So, in more graceful English, does Paul Griffith's *What the Emotions Really Are*.

Among European philosophers with an interest in neuroscience—and neuroscientists with an interest in philosophy—the most common theoretical bridge between the two fields has been phenomenology. That is the route followed here. The reader should be warned that this book does not follow what Donn Welton has called the standard interpretation of Husserl; but it follows an approach which would, I think, suggest itself to anyone who begins with Husserl's most mature works and proceeds backwards, instead of starting with the *Logical Investigations* and the first volume of *Ideas*. This "other Husserl" has not lacked for advocates in North America, beginning with David Carr's wonderfully lucid *Phenomenology and the Problem of History*. (Carr's too-few other books are similarly as pleasurable to read as they are thought-provoking.) But it was unlikely to attract adherents as long as Husserl's lectures of the 'twenties and other unpublished works were unavailable.

It was not until 2001 that an English translation of the *Analyses Concerning Active and Passive Synthesis* was published, in the very expensive Kluwer edition. The translator, Anthony Steinbock, has developed some of the implications of this work in his excellent *Home and Beyond: Generative Phenomenology after Husserl*. This book, along with Carr's text and Donn Welton's *The Other Husserl*, together provide a good orientation to this difficult but essential philosopher. The curious reader looking to explore the possible connections among phenomenology, neuroscience and cognitive science might then turn to a pair of essay collections: *Naturalizing Phenomenology*, edited by Jean Petiot, and *Les neurosciences et la philosophie de l'action*, edited by Jean-Luc Petit.

* * *

To escape the stereotypes of Periclean Athens one might go beyond the standard texts in this way: For the (essential) background in the archaic period, the path breaking work of Anthony Snodgrass and the more recent books by Robin Osborne. Then, for social history, Ellen Wood's critique of the common notion of Athens as a slave economy, which sheds needed light on the unique way in which Athenian democracy turned aristocratic norms into the practices of a far wider population. On the other end—the *far* end—of the political spectrum is Victor Davis Hanson. If one can overlook the hysteria that overcomes him whenever he thinks about Western Civilization, though, he presents a Greece that fits surprisingly well with that sketched by Wood, and he deserves credit for emphasizing the central place that warfare occupied in the *polis*.

The visual environment of the Greek city was as full of significance as the literary culture, and along with Homer—the "Bible of the Greeks"—and the great tragedians—Sophocles translates better than Aeschylus, and cuts closer to the heart of things than does Euripides—there is much to be gained from surveys such as Spivey's and Pollitt's.

This brings us to the difficult issue of Greek "mentalities." Good starting points in what has been largely a French preoccupation are the essays of Jean-Pierre Vernant and the work of Marcel Detienne. Readers who take a more Anglo-Saxon tack may be intrigued by Onians's highly individual *Origins of European Thought*. Much in E. R. Dodds's classic *The Greeks and the Irrational* has been discredited, including his speculations on shamanism, but it remains an enthralling and useful read. And the oddness of preclassical Greek ideas as well as their relevance to the kind of analysis attempted in the present work is brought out brilliantly in the late Bernard Williams's Sather Lectures, *Shame and Necessity*.

What the Greeks talked about instead of philosophy was the subject of Dover's pioneering *Greek Popular Morality*. There were, of course, philosophers to contend with. Yet here, too, there is a common misconception: that the philosophers of antiquity were concerned with disinterested speculation, like the philosophy professors of today. Instead, as Pierre Hadot has shown, ancient philosophies were spiritual disciplines, close to if not identical with the religions of the time.

If Hadot can be criticized it is for a tendency to ignore the changing status and social role of the philosopher through the many centuries between Solon and Augustine. One excellent account of these transformations, as shown through the visual arts, can be found in Paul Zanker's *The Mask of Socrates.*

Stoicism was the philosophical school with the greatest appeal to the Roman elite, and because of that we have the documents of Seneca, Epictetus and Marcus Aurelius, Stoics all, and the sympathetic treatment given the subject by Cicero. In keeping with Roman tastes, though, these prefer Stoic practice over Stoic theory. The fragments that remain of the more technical grounding of the Stoic discipline have been gathered, translated, and discussed along with the records of Epicureans and Sceptics by Long and Sedley. Long's many books on Hellenistic philosophy are valuable, though readers looking for a brief introduction may prefer Sharples's recent text.

The study of late antiquity owes an incalculable debt to Peter Brown, who all but created the period, and in an illustrated text for undergraduates, no less—*The World of Late Antiquity.* After more than thirty years it remains an important work, not least for its haunting poetry. Nothing Brown writes can be read without both pleasure and profit; the bibliography simply lists my personal favorites.

On the Christianization of the Roman Empire one might start with Ramsay MacMullen's tart little volume, Robin Lane Fox's extended narrative treatment, and the evidence of visual culture in Thomas Matthew's *The Clash of Gods.* Averill Cameron discusses the continuities between Imperial and Christian rhetoric, and the radical transformations of Christianity itself as the Empire began to crumble are treated in R.A. Markus's spellbinding *End of Ancient Christianity.* Bridging ancient and mediaeval Christianity is a difficult task for most scholars, but Caroline Walker Bynum does so in addressing a subject far more complex than may first appear, *The Resurrection of the Body.*

Before taking leave of antiquity, mention should be made of Aldo Schiavone's *The End of the Past,* a brilliant attempt to find internal reasons for the collapse of a civilization that was close to a millennium old in the days of Augustus and which many assumed would go on forever.

★ ★ ★

Nagarjuna, of course, was no more a disinterested builder of intellectual systems than were the philosophers of Western antiquity, but the extended introduction to Huntington's *The Emptiness of Emptiness* brings out the similarities between the Madhyamika and contemporary Western thought. (This cuts both ways, of course, and should remind us that Wittgenstein, to name only one, indeed saw his work as spiritual discipline.) The standard English translation of Nagarjuna's masterpiece is by Garfield, and Garfield's own essays are very helpful. Readers should be cautioned that David Kalapuhana's interpretations are accepted by few other scholars.

The distance between China and Greece is the subject of a growing number of books; it is close to a discipline it its own right. Here, as in the study of ancient Greece, French researchers have made a distinctive contribution, starting with the work of Marcel Granet and Jacques Gernet. That tradition continues today in the many books of François Jullien, only a few of which have been translated into English.

Geoffrey Lloyd, a critic of those who talk (too glibly, in his view) of "mentalities," concentrates on the structural and institutional differences between Greek and Chinese science, both in his own comparative studies and in a recent collaboration with Sinologist Nathan Sivin. Shigehisa Kuruyama treats some of the same thinkers with a very different methodology in his brilliant *The Expressiveness of the Body*. And mention should be made of the "Confucian trilogy" of David Hall and Roger Ames, from whom I borrowed the "what/how" distinction. There is much that is interesting and stimulating in their books, but they must be read with a great deal of caution. With these, even more than with most comparative studies, it is best to dip regularly into the criticisms of Haun Saussy's *Great Walls of Discourse* and Long Xi Zhang's *Mighty Opposites*.

Reservations aside, there is both a distinctive mode of thought and a distinctive vocabulary to classical Chinese thought. It is central enough that it can be approached through many different disciplines, and thus it can be a useful exercise to turn from Rudolph Wagner's recent study of a brilliant Han dynasty Taoist or A.C. Graham's now-classic study of Warring States philosophy, *Disputers of the Tao*—readers should note that his arguments from language have not worn well—to the texts collected by Steven Owen on Chinese literary thought, and from there to Kenneth DeWoskin's *A Song for One or Two*, which considers the role of music from the Han dynasty forward. (On Graham there is a very useful *festschrift* edited by Henry Rosemont.)

The bibliography on Confucianism has expanded rapidly since Herbert Fingarette's slim volume. Tu Wei-Ming has been very much the face of Confucian thought in the American academy, after Wing-Tsit Chan in the last generation, and Cheng Chung-Ying has approached the tradition with the intellectual tools of Western philosophy, not without interesting results. I leave to the reader's discretion the burgeoning recent studies on Confucianism and the family, Confucianism and ecology, Confucianism from a syncretic-Christian perspective, and many more.

For all this activity there is little valuable on Mencius. Yearly's attempt at a comparison between Mencius and Aquinas seems not to do justice to the subtlety of either man, and though the philology of Shun Kwong-Loi's *Mencius and Early Chinese Thought* is awe-inspiring, Shun seems oblivious to Mencius's ethical and political goals. There is less to criticize in Ivanhoe's slim book, but by its very nature it remains at a fairly basic level. The best recommendation is to read several different translations; Lau's edition has some helpful commentaries, and Legge's, though more than a century old, is still worth consulting, especially for its notes. Fortunately, Mencius still speaks very well for himself.

★ ★ ★

Picking through the literature on individualism is made worse by the fact that hardly any two writers mean exactly the same thing by the term. (The *Dictionary of the History of Ideas* lists no fewer than eleven "varieties of individualism.") Among the lesser-known works that I have found particularly interesting are Daniel Shanahan's wide-ranging *Toward a Genealogy of Individualism* and John Lyons's *The Invention of the Self*, which places the crucial changes in the eighteenth century—roughly the same chronology that appears in Ian Watts's celebrated *Rise of the Novel*. J.B. Schneewind's *The Invention of Autonomy*, his comprehensive "history of modern moral philosophy" also places this related though not identical event in the eighteenth century. Schneewind develops his history as an internal intellectual process, a working out of the implications of certain forms of ethical reasoning, rather than as a social transformation. It is nonetheless quite valuable both for its detailed analyses of the abandonment of providentialism and in the general movement it describes.

From a different starting point entirely comes Silvia Federici's *Caliban and the Witch: Women, the Body and Primitive Accumulation*, essential reading for anyone who hopes to make sense of the silence (and silencing) of the body under capitalism. I encountered this powerful account of what might be called the social wars of early modern Europe—against the poor and especially against women and women's knowledge—as this book was going to press. I hope some day to revisit the histories sketched here in its light.

A vivid picture of just how "advanced" Ming China was in its heyday can be found in Brook's *The Confusions of Pleasure*, which puts human and social history flesh on some of Pomerantz's economic bones. Pomerantz's work on Chinese and European economic history builds on and complements that of R. Bin Wong. Andre Gunder Frank's *ReOrient* sets out a picture of a world system dominated by China and India, presenting an alternative to received ideas of economic history; its extensive first chapter is a lively polemic against Eurocentric interpretations. A somewhat different perspective can be found in "Historical Capitalism, East and West," a lengthy paper by Giovanni Arrighi and two colleagues available on the internet. Their focus is primarily on merchant and finance capital and state power, an approach typical of the world systems theory influenced by Braudel and Wallerstein, and does not directly address the particular questions of technological innovation and industrialization that concern Pomerantz and Wong. Capitalism is indeed protean, but if one's concern is the transformation of material and social life its industrial form is incomparably the most important—a point more consistent with Pomerantz's and Frank's analyses.

Mike Davis's *Late Victorian Holocausts* details the appallingly high price India, China, and much of the rest of the world paid for their integration into the capitalist world economy.

As I was working on the final revisions to this book I encountered a short work by the psychoanalyst, philosopher, and activist Miguel Benasayag, *Le mythe de l'individu*. Benasayag's analysis uses a very different vocabulary from mine, drawing on Deleuze, Whitehead, Spinoza, and the late antique neoplatonists, and he concentrates on the atomistic, self-motivated individual as the functional basis of the neoliberal world more than on its historical genesis, but in its depth of psychological insight and passion it may serve as an important complement to the present work.

The literature on Marx is of course even larger than that on individualism, and the diversity of viewpoints even greater; yet in English, at least, there few recent works with the kind of theoretical focus that characterizes the best European Marxist scholarship. In France, for example, the reconsideration and development of Marx's insights is an undertaking within the intellectual mainstream, and it is there that some of the best contemporary analyses originate. It is good to have an English translation of Stathis Kouvelakis's superb *Philosophy and Revolution*, a study so attentive to context that it shows Heine as an important link between Hegel and Marx—beyond the intriguing fact that he was a pupil of one and a friend of the other— and which illuminates the problematic of Marx's early writings in a new way. In time, perhaps, there will be a translation of Jean-Marie

Vincent's *Un Autre Marx*, which develops the contemporary implications of that problematic and of the interdependence of subjective experience and social process which is central to Marx's vision.

Finally, for those who are encountering this approach to Marx for the first time, a recommendation: though both are old, neither Shlomo Avineri's nor Nathan Rotenstreich's books have been surpassed as introductions to Marx that take the Hegelian element seriously and yet can be understood by ordinary mortals. For the weaknesses of traditional Marxist accounts of "pre-capitalist societies" judged from a scrupulously Marxian perspective, see George Comninel's *Rethinking the French Revolution*, a work far broader in scope than its title suggests.

The best introduction to Debord in English is Anselm Jappe's *Guy Debord*, which eschews biographical melodrama (a strong temptation given Debord's self-dramatizing tendencies) in favor of placing *The Society of the Spectacle* in the context of Lukács's *History and Class Consciousness*. But Debord is little help to those looking for a way forward. A thoughtful ameliorative program has been advanced by George Monbiot in *Manifesto for a New World Order*. Miguel Benasayag, mentioned above, sees some of the same movements and others throughout the world even more positively, as germ cells of a diverse and developing social transformation which realizes its emancipatory potential in the present. Among the books in which he and different collaborators discuss issues of practice are *Résister, c'est créer* and *Du contre-pouvoir*. These books (and *Le mythe de l'individu*) are ripe for translation. But this is a subject which must be not only read about but written, and that not simply in words.

NOTES

CHAPTER 1

1 Descartes, *Meditations on First Philosophy*, II, 8, p. 174.

2 Freud, "The Unconscious," p. 576.

3 Hurley, *Consciousness in Action*, p. 12 (emphasis added).

4 Barthes, *Elements of Semiology*, I.1.2, p. 14.

5 Heidegger, *Being and Time*, 384, quoted in Sheehan, "Heidegger's New Aspect," p. 221.

6 Debord, *Society of the Spectacle*, ¶ 3.

CHAPTER 2

1 Cicero, *On Obligations*, I. 105.

2 Hurley, *Consciousness in Action*, p. 336.

3 Cicero, *Tusculan Disputations*, IV: 31.

4 Person, *Dreams of Love and Fateful Encounters*, p. 40.

5 Ibid., p. 44.

6 Bartels and Zeki, *Maternal and Romantic Love*, pp. 1163–1164.

7 Wittgenstein, *Philosophy of Psychology*, ¶ 115.

8 Buber, *I and Thou*, p. 83.

9 Damasio, *Descartes' Error*, p. 49.

10 Aurelius, *Meditations*, V, 1, p. 132.

11 Maturana and Verden-Zoller, "Biology of Love."

CHAPTER 3

1 Gardner, Mind's New Science, p. 40.

2 Gazzaniga, Ivry, and Mangun, Cognitive Neuroscience, p. 99.

3 Ibid., p. 95.

4 Jackendoff, Patterns in the Mind, p. 203.

5 Edelman and Tononi, Universe of Consciousness, pp. 93–94.

6 Wittgenstein, Philosophy of Psychology, I, ¶ 903.

7 Husserl, Crisis of European Sciences, p. 144.

8 Husserl, Pure Phenomenology, ¶ 8.

9 Husserl, Passive and Active Synthesis, p. 509.

10 Husserl, Cartesian Meditations, § 14, p. 33.

11 Husserl, Logical Investigations, p. 558 (emphasis added).

12 Husserl, Crisis of European Sciences, p. 106.

13 Ibid.

14 Ibid., p. 109.

15 Husserl, Cartesian Meditations, p. 135.

16 Husserl, Definite Determinability of Worlds, p. 544 (emph. added).

17 Husserl, Crisis of European Sciences, pp. 123–124.

18 Ibid., p. 163.

19 Clark, "Where Brain, Body, and World Collide."

20 Rizzolatti, Fogassi, and Gallese, Understanding and Imitation of Action, pp. 661–662.

21 Gallese, 'Shared Manifold' Hypothesis, pp. 37, 38.

22 Stein, Philosophy of Psychology, p. 187.

23 Pinker, Blank Slate, p. 63.

24 Gallese, Manifold Nature of Interpersonal Relations, p. 521 (emphasis in original).

25 Ibid., p. 525.

26 Husserl, Logical Investigations, p. 518.

27 Husserl, Crisis of European Man, p. 190.

28 Ramachandran, Mirror Neurons.

29 Pinker, Blank Slate, p. 434.

30 Husserl, Experience and Judgment, p. 42.

31 Ibid., pp. 31–32.

CHAPTER 4

1   Pindar, *Nemean Ode* 6: 1-7, in Pindar, *Pindar's Victory Songs.*

2   Clark, *The Nude*, p. 50.

3   Cicero, *Tusculan Disputations*, V:14.

4   Diogenes Laertius 7:49–52, in Long and Sedley,
      Hellenistic Philosophers, 39A 4–6.

5   Sextus Empiricus *Against the Professors*, 8.70, in Long &
      Sedley *Hellenistic Philosophers*, 33C.

6   Cicero, *Academica*, 2:78, in Long and Sedley,
      Hellenistic Philosophers, 40D 9.

7   Augustine, *Civ. Dei*, 8.7, in Long and Sedley, *Hellenistic
      Philosophers*, 32F.

8   Seneca, *On Anger*, 2.3.1–2.4, in Long and Sedley,
      Hellenistic Philosophers, 65Y (emphasis added).

9   Cicero, *Tusculan Disputations*, III:25.

10   Ibid., III:61 (emphasis added).

11   Ibid., III:65.

12   Diogenes Laertius 7:116, in Long and Sedley,
      Hellenistic Philosophers, 65F 2.

13   Nagarjuna, *Wisdom of the Middle Way*, 13: 8.

14   See, e.g., Garfield, *Empty Words*, pp. 46 ff.

15   Huntington and Wangchen, *Emptiness of Emptiness*, p. 107.

16   Ibid., p. 107.

17   Cicero, *Of Ends* 3:31, in Long and Sedley, *Hellenistic
      Philosophers*, 64A.

18   Diogenes Laertius 7:86, in Long and Sedley, *Hellenistic
      Philosophers*, 57A 5)

19   Cicero, *On Ends*, 3.20, 22, in Long and Sedley, *Hellenistic
      Philosophers*, 59A 4, 6.

20   Hippocrates, *Tradition in Medicine*, ¶ 3, p. 72.

21   Homer, *Iliad*, IX, pp. 497-505.

22   Cicero, *The Nature of the Gods* 1.39, in Long and Sedley,
      Hellenistic Philosophers, 54B.

23   Thucydides, *Peloponnesian War*, 5:89.

24 United States, 2002 National Security Policy.

25 Vygotsky, Thought and Language, pp. 139, 141–142.

CHAPTER 5

1   Lk 12:6–7

2   Plutarch, Oracles in Decline, ch. 10, in Plutarch, Moralia.

3   Long and Sedley, Hellenistic Philosophers, 4702; 541.

4   Plutarch, Socrates' Daimonion, ch. 1, in Plutarch, Moralia.

5   (D. 93)

6   Lyotard, Just Gaming, p. 43.

7   Heliodorus, "Ethiopian Tale," V.11.

8   Homer, Iliad, II, 573–576.

9   Plutarch, Conceptions Against the Stoics, ch. 14, in Plutarch, Moralia.

10 Aelius Aristides, Oratio XLII, 5, in Edelstein and Edelstein, Asclepius , p. 160.

11 Aelius Aristides, Oratio XLVIII, 31–35, in Edelstein and Edelstein, Asclepius, pp. 210–211.

12 Wittgenstein, Tractatus Logico-Philosophicus, 6.41.

13 Plato, Seventh Letter, 326b, in Plato, Collected Dialogues.

14 Plato, Ion, 535e, in Plato, Collected Dialogues.

15 Plato, Republic, 608a, in Plato, Collected Dialogues.

16 Plato, Timaeus, 37b-c, in Plato, Collected Dialogues.

17 Troeltsch, Social Teaching of the Christian Churches, I, 83.

18 Augustine, City of God, XIX, 18, p. 879.

19 Salisbury, Perpetua's Passion, p. 89.

CHAPTER 6

1   Carrasco, City of Sacrifice, p. 196.

2   Taylor, Sources of the Self, p. 340.

3   MacIntyre , Short History of Ethics, p. 79.

4   Rawls, Theory of Justice, p. 252.

5   Sandel, Liberalism and the Limits of Justice, p. 94.

6   Kant, Metaphysic of Morals, ak. 398-399.

7   Kant, *Lectures on Ethics*, p. 37.

8   Ibid., p. 40.

9   Taylor, *Sources of the Self*, p. 5.

10 Confucius, *Analects*, 7:16.

11 *I Ching*, pp. 55–56.

12 Mencius, *Mencius*, 2A:6.

13 Ibid.

14 Ibid., 7B:37.

15 Mencius, *Mencius* 7B:37; Confucius, *Analects*, 17:13.

16 Mencius, *Mencius*, 7A:15.

17 Ibid., 5B:1.

18 Ibid., 2A:2.

19 Ibid., 5B:1.

20 Ibid., 1A:7.

21 Ibid., 6A:8.

22 Ibid., 1A:7.

23 Ibid., 3A:5.

24 Ibid., 4A:27.

25 Jullien, *Dialogue sur la Morale*, p. 167.

26 Mencius, *Mencius*, 2A:2.

27 Ibid., 6A:10.

CHAPTER 7

1   Montesquieu, *Greatness of the Romans*, p. 25.

2   Debord, *The Society of the Spectacle*, ¶ 44.

3   Marx, *Economic and Philosophical Manuscripts*, p. 329.

CHAPTER 8

1   Marx, "British Rule in India," p. 125.

2   Debord, *Society of the Spectacle*, ¶ 87 (emphasis in original).

3   Debord, *Society of the Spectacle*, ¶ 2.

4   Marx, *Economic and Philosophical Manuscripts*, 329–330.

5   Kakar, *Inner World*, p. 107.

CHAPTER 9

1   Ginzburg, *Legends of the Jews*, I, 61.

2   Ibid., I, 86.

3   Benasayag, *Le myth de l'individu*, pp. 162–163.

4   Marx, *Theses on Feuerbach* (emphasis in original), p. 24.

5   Rotenstreich, *Basic Problems of Marx's Philosophy*, p. 59.

6   Marx, *Theses on Feuerbach*, ¶ 1.

7   Ibid., ¶¶ 9, 10.

8   Vincent, *Un Autre Marx*, p. 106 (my translation).

9   Ibid., pp. 77-78.

10 Mencius, *Mencius*, 2A:2.

11 Lévi-Strauss, *Tristes Tropiques*, p. 398 (emphasis added).

12 Ibid., p. 398.

13 Benasayag and Sztulwark, *Du contre-pouvoir*, p. 15.

14 Nietzsche, *Birth of Tragedy*, p. 72.

BIBLIOGRAPHY

Aristotle. *Nicomachean Ethics.* Translated by T. Irwin.
Indianapolis: Hackett, 1985.

Arrighi, Giovanni, Po-Keung Hui, and Ho-Fung Hung.
Historical Capitalism, East and West. www.longtermchange.net/
downloads/arrighi, hui and hung 2001 .pdf

Augustine of Hippo. *The City of God Against the Pagans.*
Translated by H. Bettenson. London: Penguin, 1972.

Avineri, Shlomo. *The Social and Political Thought of Karl Marx.*
Cambridge: Cambridge University Press, 1970.

Barthes, Roland. *Elements of Semiology.* Translated by A. Lavers
and C. Smith. New York: Hill and Wang, 1968.

Bartels, Andreas, and Semir Zeki. "The Neural Basis of
Romantic Love." *NeuroReport* 11, no. 17 (November 2000):
3829–3834.

Bartels, Andreas, and Semir Zeki. "The Neural Correlates
of Maternal and Romantic Love." *NeuroImage* 21
(2004):1155–1166.

Benasayag, Miguel. *Le mythe de l'Individu*. Translated by A. Weinfeld. Paris: La Découverte, 2004.

Benasayag, Miguel, and Florence Aubenas. *Résister, c'est créer*. Paris: La Découverte, 2002.

Benasayag, Michel, and Diego Sztulwark. *Du contre-pouvoir*. Translated by A. Weinfeld. Paris: La Découverte, 2003.

Bourdieu, Pierre. *The Logic of Practice*. Translated by R. Nice. Stanford: Stanford University Press, 1990.

Bourdieu, Pierre. *Practical Reason: On the Theory of Action*. Stanford: Stanford University Press, 1998.

Brook, Timothy. *The Confusions of Pleasure: A History of Ming China (1368–1644)*. Berkeley: University of California Press, 1998.

Brooks, E. Bruce, and A. Taeko. *The Original Analects: Sayings of Confucius and His Successors*. New York: Columbia University Press, 1998.

Brown, Peter. *Authority and the Sacred: Aspects of the Christianization of the Roman World*. Cambridge: Cambridge University Press, 1995.

Brown, Peter. *The Body and Society: Men, Women, and Sexual Renunciation in Early Christianity*. New York: Columbia University Press, 1988.

Brown, Peter. *The Cult of the Saints: Its Rise and Function in Latin Christianity*. Chicago: University of Chicago Press, 1981.

Brown, Peter. *Society and the Holy in Late Antiquity*. Berkeley: University of California Press, 1992.

Brown, Peter. *The World of Late Antiquity, A.D. 100–750*. London: Thames & Hudson, 1971.

Buber, Martin. *I and Thou*. Translated by W. Kaufmann. New York: Simon & Shuster, 1970.

Budiansky, Stephen. "Why Your Dog Pretends to Love You." *The Atlantic Monthly* 284, no. 1 (July 1999). Available under the title "The Truth About Dogs" at http://www.theatlantic.com/issues/99jul/9907dogs.htm.

Bynum, Caroline Walker. *The Resurrection of the Body in Western Christianity, 200–1336*. New York: Columbia University Press, 1995.

Cameron, Averil. *Christianity and the Rhetoric of Empire: The Development of Christian Discourse*. Berkeley: University of California Press, 1991.

Carr, David. *Phenomenology and the Problem of History: A Study of Husserl's Transcendental Philosophy*. Evanston: Northwestern University Press, 1974.

Carr, David. *The Paradox of Subjectivity: The Self in the Transcendental Tradition*. New York: Oxford University Press, 1999.

Carrasco, David. *City of Sacrifice: Violence from the Aztec Empire to the Modern Americas*. Boston: Beacon Press, 2000.

Cheng, Chung-ying. *New Dimensions of Confucian and Neo-Confucian Philosophy*. Albany: State University of New York Press, 1991.

Cicero. *On Obligations [De Officiis]*. Translated by P.G. Walsh. Oxford: Oxford University Press, 2000.

Cicero. "Tusculan Dissertations, Books III and IV." In *Cicero on the Emotions*, edited and translated by Margaret Graver. Chicago: University of Chicago Press, 2002.

Clark, Andy. "Where Brain, Body and World Collide." *Daedalus* 127, no. 2 (1998).

Clark, Kenneth. *The Nude: A Study in Ideal Form.* Garden City: Doubleday Anchor, 1956.

Comninel, George C. *Rethinking the French Revolution: Marxism and the Revisionist Challenge.* London: Verso, 1987.

Confucius. *Analects.* Translated by Charles Muller. http://www.human.toyogakuen-u.ac.jp/ffiacmuller/contao/ analects.html {see also Brooks, *supra*}.

Conze, Edward. "The Diamond Sutra." In *Buddhist Wisdom Books.* London: Allen and Unwin, 1958.

Damasio, Antonio R. *Descartes' Error: Emotion, Reason, and the Human Brain.* New York: Avon Books, 1995.

Damasio, Antonio. *The Feeling of What Happens: Body and Emotion in the Making of Consciousness.* New York: Harcourt Brace, 1999.

Davis, Mike. *Late Victorian Holocausts: El Niño Famines and the Making of the Third World.* London: Verso, 2001.

Debord, Guy. *The Society of the Spectacle.* Translated by D.Nicholson-Smith. New York: Zone Books, 1995.

Dennett, Daniel. *Consciousness Explained.* Boston: Little Brown & Co., 1991.

Descartes, Pierre. "Meditations on First Philosophy." Translated by E.S. Haldane and G.R.T. Ross. In *The Essential Descartes,* edited by M. D. Wilson. New York: New American Library Mentor Books, 1969.

Detienne, Marcel. *The Masters of Truth in Archaic Greece.* Translated by J. Lloyd. New York: Zone Books, 1995.

DeWoskin, Kenneth. *A Song for One or Two: Music and the Concept of Art in Early China.* Ann Arbor: Center for Chinese Studies, University of Michigan, 1982.

Dodds, E. R. *The Greeks and the Irrational.* Boston: Beacon Press, 1957.

Dodds, E.R. *Pagan and Christian in an Age of Anxiety: Some Aspects of Religious Experience from Marcus Aurelius to Constantine.* New York: Norton, 1970.

Dover, K.J. *Greek Popular Morality in the Time of Plato and Aristotle.* Indianapolis: Hackett, 1994.

Edelman, Gerald M. *Bright Air, Brilliant Fire: On the Matter of the Mind.* New York: Basic Books, 1992.

Edelman, Gerald M. *The Remembered Present: A Biological Theory of Consciousness.* New York: Basic Books, 1989.

Edelman, Gerald M. *Neural Darwinism: The Theory of Neuronal Group Selection.* New York: Basic Books, 1987.

Edelman, Gerald, and Giulio Tononi. *A Universe of Consciousness: How Matter Becomes Imagination.* New York: Basic Books, 2000.

Edelstein, Emma J., and Ludwig Edelstein. *Asclepius: Collection and Interpretation of the Testimonies.* Baltimore: Johns Hopkins University Press, 1998.

Edwards, Paul N. *The Closed World: Computers and the Politics of Discourse in Cold War America.* Cambridge: MIT Press, 1996.

Federici, Silvia. *Caliban and the Witch: Women, the Body and Primitive Accumulation.* New York: Autonomedia, 2004.

Fingarette, Herbert. *Confucius—The Secular as Sacred.* New York: Harper & Row, 1962.

Fox, Robin Lane. *Pagans and Christians*. San Francisco: Harper & Row, 1986.

Frank, Andre Gunder. *ReOrient: Global Economy in the Asian Age*. Berkeley: University of California Press, 1998.

Freud, Sigmund. "The Unconscious." In *The Freud Reader*, edited by P. Gay. New York: Norton, 1989.

Gallese, Vittorio. "The Manifold Nature of Interpersonal Relations: The Quest for a Common Mechanism." *Phil. Trans. Royal Soc. London* 358, no. 1431 (2003):517–528.

Gallese, Vittorio. "The 'Shared Manifold' Hypothesis: From Mirror Neurons to Empathy." *Journal of Consciousness Studies* 8, no. 5–7 (2001):33–50.

Gardner, Howard. *The Mind's New Science: A History of the Cognitive Revolution*. New York: Basic Books, 1987.

Garfield, Jay L. *Empty Words: Buddhist Philosophy and Cross-Cultural Interpretation*. Oxford: Oxford University Press, 2002.

Gazzaniga, Michael, Richard Ivry, and George Mangun. *Cognitive Neuroscience: The Biology of the Mind*. New York: Norton, 1998.

Gernet, Jacques. *China and the Christian Impact*. Translated by J. Lloyd. Cambridge: Cambridge University Press, 1985.

Ginzburg, Louis. *The Legends of the Jews: Vol. I, From the Creation to Jacob*. Translated by H. Szold. Baltimore: Johns Hopkins University Press, 1998.

Graham, A. C. *Disputers of the Tao: Philosophical Argument in Ancient China*. LaSalle, Ill.: Open Court, 1989.

Graham, A.C. *Reason and Spontaneity: A new solution to the problem of fact and value*. London: Curzon Press, and Totowa: Barnes & Noble, 1985.

Granet, Marcel. *La Pensée Chinoise*. Paris: Éditions Albin Michel, 1968.

Griffiths, Paul. *What Emotions Really Are: The Problem of Psychological Categories*. Chicago: University of Chicago Press, 1996.

Hadot, Pierre. *Philosophy as a Way of Life*. Translated by M. Chase. Oxford: Blackwell, 1995.

Hadot, Pierre. *What is Ancient Philosophy?* Translated by M. Chase. Cambridge: Harvard University Press, 2002.

Hall, David L., and Roger T. Ames. *Anticipating China: Thinking through the Narratives of Chinese and Western Cultures*. Albany: SUNY Press, 1995.

Hall, David L., and Roger T. Ames. *Thinking from the Han: Self, Truth and Transcendence in Chinese and Western Cultures*. Albany: SUNY Press, 1998.

Hall, David L., and Roger T. Ames. *Thinking Through Confucius*. Albany: SUNY Press, 1987.

Hanson, Victor Davis. *The Other Greeks: The Family Farm and the Agrarian Roots of Western Civilization*. Berkeley: University of California Press, 1999.

Heidegger, Martin. *Being and Time*. Translated by J. McQuarrie and E. Robinson. New York: Harper & Row, 1962.

Heliodorus. "An Ethiopian Tale." Translated by J. R. Morgan. In *Collected Ancient Greek Novels*, edited by B.P. Reardon. Berkeley: University of California Press, 1989.

Hippocrates. "Tradition in Medicine". Translated by
J. Chadwick, W.N. Mann et al. In *Hippocratic Writings*, edited
by G.E.R. Lloyd. London: Penguin Books, 1978.

Homer. *The Iliad*. Translated by R. Fagles. New York:
Penguin Books, 1991.

Honderich, Ted, ed. *The Oxford Companion to Philosophy*.
Oxford: Oxford University Press, 1995.

Huntington, C.W. Jr., and Geshé Namgyal Wangchen.
*The Emptiness of Emptiness: An Introduction to Early Indian
Madhyamika*. Honolulu: University of Hawaii Press, 1989.

Hurley, Susan. *Consciousness in Action*. Cambridge: Harvard
University Press, 1998.

Husserl, Edmund. *Analyses Concerning Passive and Active
Synthesis*. Translated by A. J. Steinbock. Dordrecht:
Kluwer Academic Publishers, 2001.

Husserl, Edmund. *Cartesian Meditations*. Translated by D.
Cairns. The Hague: Martinus Nijhoff, 1960.

Husserl, Edmund. *The Crisis of European Sciences and
Transcendental Philosophy*. Translated by D. Carr. Evanston:
Northwestern University Press, 1970.

Husserl, Edmund. *Experience and Judgment*. Edited by
L. Landgrebe. Translated by J.S. Churchill and K. Americks.
Evanston: Northwestern University Press, 1973.

Husserl, Edmund. *Logical Investigations*. Translated by J.N.
Findlay. Amherst, NY: Humanity Books, 2000.

Husserl, Edmund. "Pure Phenomenology, its Method
and its Field of Investigation. " Translated by R.W. Jordan.
In Husserl: Shorter Works, edited by Peter McCormick
and Frederick A. Elliston. Notre Dame, Ind.: University
of Notre Dame Press, 1981.

Husserl, Edmund. "Philosophy and the Crisis of European
Man." Translated by Q. Lauer. In Edmund Husserl,
Phenomenology and the Crisis of Philosophy. New York: Harper &
Row, 1965.

[I Ching] The Classic of Changes: A New Translation of the I Ching
as Interpreted by Wang Bi. Translated by Richard John Lynn.
New York: Columbia University Press, 1994.

Ivanhoe, Philip J. Ethics in the Confucian Tradition: The Thought of
Mencius and Wang Yang-Ming. Atlanta: Scholars Press, 1990.

Jackendoff, Ray. Patterns in the Mind: Language and Human
Nature. New York: Basic Books, 1994.

Jappe, Anselm. Guy Debord. Translated by D. Nicholson-
Smith. Berkeley: University of California Press, 1993.

Jullien, François. Detour and Access: Strategies of Meaning
in China and Greece. Translated by S. Hawkes. New York:
Zone Books, 2000.

Jullien, François. Dialogue sur la Morale. Paris: Grasset, 1995.

Jullien, François. The Propensity of Things: Towards a History
of Efficacy in China. Translated by J. Lloyd. New York:
Zone Books, 1999.

Kakar, Sudhir. The Inner World: A Psycho-analytic Study of Childhood and Society in India. Delhi: Oxford University Press, 1981.

Kant, Immanuel. *Grounding for the Metaphysic of Morals.*
Translated by J.W. Ellington. Indianapolis: Hackett, 1994.

Kant, Immanuel. *Lectures on Ethics.* Translated by L. Infield.
New York: Harper & Row, 1963.

Keil, Frank. *Concepts, Kinds and Cognitive Development.*
Cambridge, Mass.: MIT Press, 1992.

Kouvelakis, Stathis. *Philosophy and Revolution; From Kant to
Marx.* Translated by G.M. Goshgarian. London: Verso, 2003.

Kuruyama, Shigehisa. *The Expressiveness of the Body and the
Divergence of Greek and Chinese Medicine.* New York:
Zone Books, 1999.

Lévi-Strauss, Claude. *Tristes Tropiques.* Translated by J. Russell.
New York: Atheneum, 1967.

Lévi-Strauss, Claude. *The Savage Mind.* Chicago: University
of Chicago Press, 1966.

Lévi-Strauss, Claude. *Structural Anthropology.* Translated by C.
Jacobson and B.G. Schoepf. New York: Anchor Books, 1967.

Lewontin, Richard. *The Triple Helix: Gene, Organism and
Environment.* Cambridge: Harvard University Press, 2000.

Libert, Benjamin. *Mind Time: The Temporal Dimensions of
Consciousness.* Cambridge: Harvard University Press, 2004.

Lloyd, G.E.R. *Adversaries and Authorities: Investigations into
Ancient Greek and Chinese Science.* Cambridge: Cambridge
University Press, 1995.

Lloyd, Geoffrey and Nathan Sivin. *The Way and the Word:
Science and Medicine in Early China and Greece.* New Haven:
Yale University Press, 2002.

Long, A.A. *Hellenistic Philosophy: Stoics, Epicureans, Sceptics.*
2nd ed. Berkeley: University of California Press, 1986.

Long, A.A. *Stoic Studies.* Berkeley: University of California
Press, 1996.

Long, A.A., and D.N. Sedley, ed. *The Hellenistic Philosophers.*
(2 vols.) Cambridge: Cambridge University Press, 1987.

Long, Xi Zhang. *Mighty Opposites: From Dichotomy to Difference
in the Comparative Study of China.* Stanford: Stanford
University Press, 1998.

Lukács, Georg. *History and Class Consciousness: Studies
in Marxist Dialectics.* Translated by R. Livingstone. Cambridge:
MIT Press, 1971.

Lyons, John O. *The Invention of the Self: The Hinge of
Consciousness in the Eighteenth Century.* Carbondale: Southern
Illinois University Press, 1978.

Lyotard, Jean-François and Jean-Loup Thébaud. *Just Gaming.*
Translated by W. Godzich. Minneapolis: University
of Minnesota Press, 1985.

MacMullen, Ramsay. *Christianizing the Roman Empire, A.D.
100–400.* New Haven: Yale University Press, 1981.

MacIntyre, Alasdair. *A Short History of Ethics.* New York:
Macmillan, 1966.

Marcus Aurelius. "Meditations." Translated by G. Long.
In *Essential Works of Stoicism,* edited by M. Hadas. New York:
Bantam Books, 1961.

Markus, R.A. *The End of Ancient Christianity.* Cambridge:
Cambridge University Press, 1990.

Marx, Karl. "Economic and Philosophical Manuscripts of 1844." Translated by G. Benton. In Karl Marx, Early Writings, edited by Q. Hoare. New York: Vintage, 1975.

Marx, Karl. Theses on Feuerbach. In N. Rotenstreich. Basic Problems of Marx's Philosophy. Indianapolis: Bobbs-Merrill, 1965.

Marx, Karl. "The British Rule in India". In K. Marx and F. Engels, Collected Works. Volume 12. New York: International Publishers, 1979.

Mathews, Thomas F. The Clash of Gods: A Reinterpretation of Early Christian Art. Princeton: Princeton University Press, rev. ed., 1999.

Maturana, Humberto and Francisco Varela. Autopoiesis and Cognition: The Realization of the Living. Dordrecht: D. Reidel, 1986.

Maturana, Humberto, and Francisco Varela. The Tree of Knowledge: The Biological Roots of Human Understanding. Boston: Shambhala, 1998.

Maturana, Humberto, and Gerda Verden-Zoller. "The Biology of Love". http://members.ozemail.com.au/ffijcull/articles/bol.htm

Megill, Allan. Karl Marx: The Burden of Reason. Lanham, Md.: Rowman & Littlefield, 2002.

Mencius. Mencius. Translated by D.C. Lau. London: Penguin Books, 1970.

Mencius. The Works of Mencius. Translated by J. Legge. New York: Dover, 1970.

Mencius (selections), Translated by C. Muller. http://www.human.toyogakuen-u.ac.jp/ffiacmuller/contao/ mencius.htm

Midgely, Mary. *The Ethical Primate: Humans, Freedom and Morality.* London: Routledge, 1994.

Monbiot, George. *Manifesto for a New World Order.* New York: New Press, 2004.

Montesquieu, Charles Secondat, Baron de. *Considerations on the Causes of the Greatness of the Romans and their Decline.* Translated by D. Lowenthal. Ithaca: Cornell University Press, 1968.

Nagarjuna. *The Fundamental Wisdom of the Middle Way.* Translated by J.L. Garfield. Oxford: Oxford University Press, 1995.

Nagel, Thomas. "What is it Like to Be a Bat?" *The Philosophical Review* LXXXIII, no. 4 (October 1974): 435-50.

Naipaul, V.S. *India: A Wounded Civilization.* New York: Knopf, 1977.

Nietzsche, Friedrich. "The Birth of Tragedy". Translated by W. Kaufmann. In *Basic Writings of Nietzsche*, edited by W. Kaufmann. New York: Modern Library, 1968.

Nørretranders, Tor. *The User Illusion: Cutting Consciousness Down to Size.* Translated by J. Sydenham. New York: Viking, 1998.

Onians, R. B. *The Origins of European Thought about the Body, the Mind, the Soul, the World, Time and Fate.* Cambridge: Cambridge University Press, 1988.

Osborne, Robin. *Greece in the Making, 1200–479 BC.* London: Routledge, 1996.

Owen, Stephen. *Readings in Chinese Literary Thought.* Cambridge: Harvard University Press, 1992.

Oyama, Susan. *The Ontogeny of Information: Developmental Systems and Evolution.* Durham, NC: Duke University Press, 2000.

Oyama, Susan. *Evolution's Eye: A Systems View of the Biology–Culture Divide*. Durham, NC: Duke University Press, 2000.

Person, Ethel. *Dreams of Love and Fateful Encounters: The Power of Romantic Passion*. New York: Penguin Books, 1989.

Petiot, Jean, et al., eds. *Naturalizing Phenomenology: Issues in contemporary phenomenology and cognitive science*. Stanford: Stanford University Press, 1999.

Petit, Jean-Luc, ed. *Les neurosciences et la philosophie de l'action*. Paris: J. Vrin, 1997.

Pindar. *Pindar's Victory Songs*. Translated by F.J. Nisetich. Baltimore: Johns Hopkins University Press, 1980.

Pinker, Stephen. *The Blank Slate: The Modern Denial of Human Nature*. New York: Penguin Books, 2002.

Plato. *Collected Dialogues, including the Letters*. Edited by E. Hamilton and H. Cairns. Princeton: Princeton University Press, 1961.

Plutarch. *Miscellanies and Essays* [Moralia]. Edited by W. Goodwin. Boston: Little, Brown & Co., 1898.

Pollitt, J.J. *Art and Experience in Classical Greece*. Cambridge: Cambridge University Press, 1972.

Pomeranz, Kenneth. *The Great Divergence: China, Europe, and the Making of the Modern World Economy*. Princeton: Princeton University Press, 2000.

Ramachandran, V.S. "Mirror neurons and imitation learning," *Edge* 69, 2000, http://www.edge.org/3rd_culture/ramachandran/ramachandran_index.html.

Ramachandran, V.S., and Sandra Blakeslee. *Phantoms in the Brain: Probing the Mysteries of the Human Mind*. New York: William Murrow, 1998.

Rawls, John. *A Theory of Justice*. Cambridge: Harvard University Press, 1971.

Rizzolatti, Giacomo, Leonardo Fogassi, and Vittorio Gallese. "Neurophysiological Mechanisms Underlying the Understanding and Imitation of Action." *Nature Reviews: Neuroscience* 2 (2001):661–670.

Rosemont, Henry, ed. *Chinese Texts and Philosophical Contexts: Essays dedicated to Angus C. Graham*. LaSalle, Ill.: Open Court, 1991.

Rotenstreich, Nathan. *Basic Problems of Marx's Philosophy*. Indianapolis: Bobbs-Merrill, 1965.

Salisbury, Joyce E. *Perpetua's Passion: The Death and Memory of a Young Roman Woman*. New York: Routledge, 1997.

Sandel, Michael. *Liberalism and the Limits of Justice*. Cambridge: Cambridge University Press, 1982.

Saussy, Haun. *Great Walls of Discourse and Other Adventures in Cultural China*. Cambridge: Harvard University Press, 2001.

Saussure, Ferdinand de. *Course in General Linguistcs*. Translated by Baskin, W. New York: McGraw-Hill, 1966.

Schiavone, Aldo. *The End of the Past: Ancient Rome and the Modern West*. Translated by M.J. Schneider. Cambridge: Harvard University Press, 2000.

Shanahan, Daniel. *Toward a Genealogy of Individualism*. Amherst: University of Massachusetts Press, 1992.

Sharples, R.W. *Stoics, Epicureans and Sceptics: An Introduction to Hellenistic Philosophy.* London: Routledge, 1996.

Sheehan, Thomas. "Heidegger's New Aspect: On In-Sein, Zeitlichkeit, and The Genesis of 'Being and Time.'"*Research in Phenomenology* 25 (November 1995), pp. 207–225.

Schneewind, J.B. *The Invention of Autonomy: A History of Modern Moral Philosophy.* Cambridge: Cambridge University Press, 1998.

Shun, Kwong-Loi. *Mencius and Early Chinese Thought.* Stanford: Stanford University Press, 1997.

Snodgrass, Anthony. *Archaic Greece: The Age of Experiment.* Berkeley: University of California Press, 1980.

Spivey, Nigel. *Understanding Greek Sculpture: Ancient Meanings, Modern Readings.* London: Thames & Hudson, 1995.

Stein, Edith. *Philosophy of Psychology and the Humanities.* Translated by M.C. Baseheart and M. Sawicki. Washington, DC: Institute of Carmelite Studies, 2000.

Steinbock, Anthony. *Home and Beyond: Generative Phenomenology after Husserl.* Evanston: Northwestern University Press, 1995.

Taylor, Charles. *Sources of the Self: The Making of the Modern Identity.* Cambridge: Harvard University Press, 1989.

Thornton, John. *Africa and Africans in the Making of the Atlantic World, 1400–1800.* 2nd ed. Cambridge: Cambridge University Press, 1998.

Thucydides. *The Peloponnesian War.* Edited by R. Strassler. Translated by R. Crawley. New York: Simon & Schuster, 1996.

Troeltsch, Ernst. *The Social Teaching of the Christian Churches* (2 volumes). Translated by O. Wyon. Louisville, Westminster/John Knox, 1992.

Tu Wei-Ming. *Confucian Thought: Selfhood as Creative Transformation.* Albany: State University of New York Press, 1985.

Ulansey, David. *The Origins of the Mithraic Mysteries.* Oxford: Oxford University Press, 1991.

Vakaloulis, Michel, Jean-Marie Vincent, and Pierre Zarka. *Vers un nouvel anticapitalisme: Pour une politique d'émancipation.* Paris: Éditions du félin, 2003.

Varela, Francisco J., Evan Thompson, and Eleanor Rosch. *The Embodied Mind: Cognitive Science and Human Experience.* Cambridge: The MIT Press, 1993.

Vernant, Jean-Pierre. *Mortals and Immortals: Collected Essays.* Edited by F. Zeitlin. Princeton: Princeton University Press, 1991.

Vernant, Jean-Pierre. *Myth and Society in Ancient Greece.* Translated by J. Lloyd. London: Methuen, 1982.

Vernant, Jean-Pierre. *The Origins of Greek Thought.* Ithaca: Cornell University Press, 1984.

Vernant, Jean-Pierre, and Pierre Vidal-Naquet. *Myth and Tragedy in Ancient Greece.* Translated by J. Lloyd. New York: Zone Books, 1990.

Vincent, Jean-Marie. *Un Autre Marx: Après les Marxismes.* Lausanne: Éditions page deux, 2001.

Vygotsky, Lev Semyonovich. *Thought and Language.* Translated by E. Henfmann & G. Vakar. Cambridge: The M.I.T. Press, 1962.

Vygotsky, Lev Semyonovich. *Mind in Society: The Development of Higher Psychological Processes*. Translated by M. Lopez-Morillas and M. Cole. Cambridge: Harvard University Press, 1978.

Wagner, Rudolf G. *Language, Ontology, and Political Philosophy in China: Wand Bi's Scholarly Exploration of the Dark [Xuanxue]*. Albany: State University of New York Press, 2003.

Wegner, Daniel M. *The Illusion of Conscious Will*. Cambridge: MIT Press, 2002.

Welton, Donn. *The Other Husserl: The Horizons of Transcendental Philosophy*. Bloomington: Indiana University Press, 2000.

Williams, Bernard. *Shame and Necessity*. Berkeley: University of California Press, 1993.

Wittgenstein, Ludwig. *Philosophical Investigations*. 3rd edition. Translated by G.E.M. Anscombe. New York: Macmillan, 1958.

Wittgenstein, Ludwig. *Tractatus Logico-Philosophicus*. Translated by D.F. Pears and B.F. McGuinness. London: Routledge, 1974.

Wittgenstein, Ludwig. *Remarks on the Philosophy of Psychology*. Translated by G.E.M. Anscombe. Chicago: University of Chicago Press, 1980.

Wong, R. Bin. *China Transformed: Historical Change and the Limits of European Experience*. Ithaca: Cornell University Press, 1997.

Wood, Ellen Meiksins. *Peasant Citizen and Slave: The Foundations of Athenian Democracy*. London: Verso, 1989.

Yearley, Lee H. *Mencius and Aquinas: Theories of Virtue and Conceptions of Courage*. Albany: State University of New York Press, 1990.

Zanker, Paul. *The Mask of Socrates; The Image of the Intellectual in Antiquity*. Translated by A. Shapiro. Berkeley: California University Press, 1995.

INDEX